WHAT EVERY WORKING WOMAN NEEDS TO KNOW

...AND DO

First published in 2008 by

CURRACH PRESS

55A Spruce Avenue, Stillorgan Industrial Park, Blackrock, Co. Dublin

www.currach.ie

1 3 5 4 2

Cover by sin é design

Origination by Currach Press

Printed in Ireland by ColourBooks, Baldoyle Industrial Estate, Dublin 13

ISBN: 978-1-85607-972-3

What Every Working Woman Needs to Know

...and Do

Terry Prone

CURRACH
PRESS

ACKNOWLEDGEMENTS

Everybody in the Communications Clinic contributed to this book. Gratitude goes to Chairman, Tom Savage, and Managing Director, Anton Savage, Stephanie Brady, who keeps the Clinic show on the road, Eoghan McDermott, who heads up the Career Clinic, Hilary Kenny, who does ditto for the Training Clinic, Gerard Kenny and Ruth (Ruthless) Hickey who run our PR Clinic, Breda Fox, Ailish Smith, Karagh Fox, Taunya Gibney and Karla Sloyan.

Mary Hosty, novelist and teacher, generously gave time and insight, as did Paige Crosbie and another friend who doesn't want to be named.

Portions of this book appeared in different form in the *Irish Examiner*, the *Sunday Independent*, the *Daily Mail*, the *Evening Herald*, the *Sunday Mail* and *Image* magazine. Many thanks to the editors for commissioning the original features and permitting their re-use.

CONTENTS

INTRODUCTION

You're an accountant. Or a nurse. Or you work in a dry-cleaners.

You're a solicitor in a provincial town.

Or a barrister in the Law Library.

You're a taxi driver. Or a teacher. Or a CEO. Or a PR account manager. Or you've never had a job or are between jobs.

You're a daughter, a partner, a sin5gle woman or a mother. Or you've been all four.

You juggle a million things every day, and you wonder if other working women have secrets to which you're not privy. Or hints that could help your progress. Or warnings that could prevent you falling into a career pothole.

That's where this book started. With two working women. One is a publisher, the other a writer who's also a business-woman.

Jo O'Donoghue is an historian, an editor and publisher at Currach Press. Terry Prone (that's me) is a Director of the Communications Clinic and has published twenty-six books. We met each other more than twenty years ago, when Jo edited one of my early books. Since then, roughly every eighteen months, Jo gets an idea for a book I should write. In 2008, the idea was for a book that would be useful to working women. Maybe open up possibilities for greater fulfilment and happiness.

You hold the result in your hand. Jo and I hope it'll be useful to you. And that you'll come back to chapters within it in a year. Or two years. Or ten years' time. Just as you'd go back to a woman friend when you need a dig-out.

Terry Prone, 2008

1

What Do Working Women Want to Know?

You say 'women are more sympathetic than men'. Now if I were to write a book out of my experience, I should begin, Women have no sympathy. Yours is the tradition – mine is the conviction of experience. I have never found one woman who has altered her life by one iota for me or my opinions.

Florence Nightingale

Before setting out to find out from working women what they'd want to ask successful women, I did a pilot. It was amazingly cost-effective.

'Oy, everybody,' I said in our open-plan office. 'What are the three questions you'd like to ask successful working women?'

'How to lose weight,' one of the women said. (This summer, we did a collective diet, so food was a constant obsession.)

'Why would I want to ask successful women anything?' one of the guys said, genuinely mystified. Several of the women immediately got dug out of him. 'You think you couldn't learn from successful women?' one of them demanded.

'I learn from the successful women around me every day,' he said virtuously. Someone threw a bit of balled-up typing paper at him and suggested that if he learned from us, it was ay-mazing he hadn't learned a bog-standard skill like filling the dishwasher.

'What do you, as working women, need to know?' I clarified. 'From successful working women?'

The guy who won't use the dishwasher slunk out the door at this point.

'Depends on your definition of "successful",' the remaining guy offered. 'Does it mean she's CEO or chairman or president or that she's paid a fortune, or that she has six teenagers none of whom have yet gone to jail? Is it that she's happy or really well-paid or gets to travel a lot or has a – a – a –'

'Trophy partner?'

'I was actually thinking of a timeshare, but that, too. I mean, we all know what a successful working man looks like. He's Denis O'Brien or Michael O'Leary or Eugene Sheehy or Ivan Yates or Terence O'Rourke.'

Someone qualified this list by mentioning a feature that had recently appeared in a newspaper where Ivan Yates had announced the recession had his business – Celtic Bookmakers – by the whatsits and he was going to have to take on lots of high-paying high-prestige directorships to keep himself in the style to which his business had accustomed him. Only Ivan could get a newspaper to pay him for whingeing about being broke and doing a hard sell on himself.

'Eugene Sheehy has nothing in common with Michael O'Leary,' I opined. (I met AIB's top man once, for maybe seven pleasant minutes, so that makes me an expert. I've never met Michael O'Leary and would have to get into training to survive an encounter with him.)

The response from the group was that no successful working woman was like any other successful working woman, either. Having just been a judge for *Image* magazine of their Businesswoman of the Year competition, I slightly doubted that. *Image* had sent me a folder the size of a personhole cover containing laminated sections on each of the contenders. They were all worth millions, all (according to the testimonials produced by their friends/spouses/colleagues/staff) adorable, all awash in children and Labradors and charities to which they devoted their spare time (of which they had none), all slim, attractive and fitter than the average yak. Just reading about them made me feel inadequate – and I was a judge. (See the end of this chapter for the results of the competition.)

Our female staff, however, didn't think there'd be much point in asking such woman about their secrets. 'You couldn't ask people like Danuta Gray or Mary Finan what you'd really want to ask them,' one of the women said resignedly.

'What would you really want to ask them?'

She mouthed, 'How to lose weight' at me.

'And while I was at it, I'd want to ask them how they'd stop their mothers giving your two-year-old sugary crap while babysitting.'

'Why would their mothers be minding your kid?' the dishwasher-avoider wanted to know as he returned to the room.

'No – minding their own grandchildren. I bet they didn't, anyway. High powered women like them probably had live-in nannies. One for night-time, one for daytime and one for the weekend.'

People were beginning to drift back to their work, one of the younger women saying that if she wanted to know something about working women, she'd ask her mother, who was her best pal and a rock of sense.

One of the two men did an ironic 'Aaaah' of approval over her being so pleasant about her mother, she got shirty over him not taking her seriously, clients began to arrive and I thought my request had gone nowhere. But that afternoon, I got an e-mail from the two of them, containing the following questions they'd want asked of successful working women, however 'success' was defined:

- What has been the driving force for you? Money? Status? Power?
- Has your family life suffered as a result of your success?
- What do you love most about your job?
- What has made you successful?

When I cast my net wider, I found a significant difference between the questions younger women wanted posed and those asked by older women.

Women in their thirties wanted to know how successful women coped with stress, with unspoken anti-feminism in the workplace ('Why do you think women are stereotyped as less effective than men, or inferior to men, in the workplace?' came from Tracy Brennan, my American literary agent) and with the terror of making presentations.

Women in their forties wanted to know about the successful woman's worst setbacks, disappointments and regrets. Along the way, individual women asked questions about whether successful women liked or trusted other women, thought they were easier to get along with than men were, less or more violent than men and were more or less likely to bully and sexually harass than men. One (in her thirties) wanted to know if successful women had much of a sex life, and one (in her forties) wanted a list of the time-saving tricks used by successful women.

Not one of the women I asked claimed to be motivated by money, status or power, although they had achieved all three. Indeed, they tended to be floored by the possibility that any of the three would be career-drivers.

'I've always wanted to be in control of my own life,' one CEO told me. 'The consequence of that is running a business employing several thousand people, which theoretically means I'm powerful. But power wasn't the objective. Power was the spin-off. Control was the objective. I am heavily influenced by my late father, who basically believed that I could run the world. I never wanted to be in a job that bored or frustrated me, so as soon as I could, I got into managing projects, so I could shape what I did.'

Before you dismiss boredom-avoidance as a career-driver, consider this. One survey of English executives found that more than half of them found their jobs boring, and eight out of ten of them were bored at work at some point. Tough, you may say. But the reality is that boredom contributes to many of the problems besetting working women ranging from obesity to alcoholism. If your work bores you, it could bore you to death, since you have a greatly increased chance of cardiovascular illness, gastrointestinal disorders and stress-related absences from work. In Sweden it was found that six out of ten workers in a particularly routine and repetitive job suffered peptic ulcers at a level way above the likely occurrence in people who weren't bored.

Being in control of your own destiny is arguably the most effective way of avoiding boredom. Some women get to this point by reaching the top of a big corporation. Some by setting up their own business. Others do it by freelancing. One nurse defines the point at which she knew she was in charge of her own life as the day she moved from employment within an acute hospital to working as an agency nurse:

> In the hospital, everything was decided for me. I was a cog in a big wheel. Just another number, solving the roster problems of the day. As an agency nurse, on the other hand, I could choose to do whichever kind of work I liked, and I could choose how much of that work I did. I discovered I really liked night-work with terminal cancer patients. Yes, it was demanding, but it was so rewarding, to know I could make a difference to the comfort of someone in their last days. Just by taking care of little things. Just by listening. Just by being with them through the dark hours. I would often work in someone's home for several weeks or even months. I didn't have to do any form-filling or meetings. Just the real stuff. The stuff that made a difference.

When successful women talk about money, they tend to talk about it in utilitarian terms. It matters because of what it can *do*, not because they get a kick out of earning a quarter of a million a year. Many of them describe money as buying them freedom. Freedom from commuting, through the purchase of an expensive townhouse. Freedom from worry about childcare, by employing full-time staff. Freedom from guilt, because they are able to contribute financially to the amelioration of family problems.

Freedom even – believe it or not – from shopping, as witness a woman of my acquaintance:

One year, when I spoke at a women's networking conference, I came across the concept of the concierge. The person you can ring up and say 'I need a lovely personal present for a new baby boy,' and they'll go off and get you something perfect. Or the person you can hire to find the best nursing home for your mother, or the best hotel in Athens and flight to it.

It's back to boredom-avoidance. It was worth it to her to buy her way out of the tedium.

None of which explains how women who are lawyers and accountants strive so hard to 'make partner' while still claiming not to be motivated by status or power. They tend to explain the inconsistency by saying they're as good as anybody else in the firm and therefore should be a partner. (In other words, it's not that I need status, it's that I deserve it and would be failing my own expertise if I didn't go after it.) Or they state that making partner allows them to choose the tasks they undertake, thus putting them more in control, ergo helping them avoid boring, unchallenging or poorly-paid work. Or being answerable to someone they don't rate.

'It's the difference between primary motivator and secondary motivator,' one accountant maintains. 'My primary motivation is to do exciting work, to travel, to be taken seriously. But I honestly think I'd achieved all these before I was made partner. Making partner, for me, was the cherry on top of the cake.'

Much the same is true of Norah Casey, who owns and runs the publishing house, Harmonia, which brings out titles like *U*, *Irish Tatler*, *Woman's Way* and Diarmuid Gavin's *Garden Designs*.

She started her career as a nurse, getting an extra qualification in nursing burn victims as a way of quelling her own fear of the damage done by fire. Then she took a sideways move into a journalism course which led her into medical publishing – a logical step – and from there into magazine arm of the Smurfit company.

Norah tells her story in *That'll Never Work,* published by KPMG/Mercier, an account of the entrepreneurs who run some of Ireland's most successful indigenous businesses. It's a fascinating story, not least because, while she learned to like being in power once she became the boss of an organisation, it wasn't something she'd always wanted:

> I really couldn't believe that I could have a passion for the spreadsheets and the planning involved in business. Here I was in my twenties, a CEO getting a right kick out of the fact that I could launch a magazine and turn it around or make a business decision that would have an impact on the bottom line.

There's an interesting disconnect between the women who reach the top level, whether in self-started, indigenous, multi-national or state-sponsored organisations, and women who are happy at the lower rungs. The majority of women rate a company highly if they're kept in the loop about what's going on, if the company is good about career-planning and maternity provisions and – in all its works and pomps – is fair and equitable. Tom Savage, who undertakes communications audits in commercial companies and state-sponsored bodies, has found, over the past ten years, that the most frequent complaint by staff is a version of 'Nobody ever tells us anything.' In too many companies, the grapevine is a better source of information than the management.

Women at the top, on the other hand, prioritise excitement, change, challenge, promotion possibilities and travel. Clearly, the choices made by happy working women at the lower levels in such organisations, particularly if they work-share, relate to their family choices. Women who reach the top are more likely to be single, divorced or childless, although the numbers are not sufficiently stark as to invite the judgement that if you want to get to the top, you should steer clear of having a significant other or a bunch of children.

Asked if their career success had in any way dented their family life, most of the successful women immediately and crossly said it hadn't. Several immediately added that a man wouldn't be asked that question. One of them said:

> When my daughter had croup, I sat up through the night with her and then went to work. The difference is that – like a man – I didn't talk about it. I just did it. What's with this idea that if you're promoted, you're somehow immune to all the hassles 'ordinary' women have? We all experience miscarriages, relationship breakups, mad relatives, illnesses, burst pipes and lost dry cleaning. We just manage them without whining. And if that makes me sound like a bitch, tough. I think an awful lot of not-very-competent women let themselves off the hook by saying they couldn't devote the time to the job because their children would've suffered. So they take a career break and sit at home eating muffins and watching that purple alligator thing with their toddler.

(She's got her species wrong. She means Barney, the purple dinosaur.)

Her point, forcefully made, is that if you can't manage domestic crises, you can't manage anything. Another managing director who bristled at the question said that it derived from what she called the 'female guilt-trip'. Men were not stereotyped as 'the right person' to take care of children, she pointed out, and therefore didn't: a) get asked the question; or b) feel guilty about not being home making cookies every afternoon. She said crisply:

> I realised, early in my career, that I wanted no part of the female guilt trip. Women who sit around at work saying they feel so guilty that they can't be at the graduation ceremony of their toddler from kindergarten. *Puhlease.* Four-year-olds running around in caps and gowns and being described by idiot mothers as 'so cute'. Like it matters that you didn't turn up for something so sickening. Like it affects your child's health and happiness in any way. Like you actually should dignify that kind of crap with your presence. That and bouncing castles. I have nothing in common with any mother who would hire a bouncing castle for her kid's birthday. Nothing. Not only will I not feel guilty that my twins didn't have bouncing castles, I'll know that they were bouncing-castled up to their ears at other kids' birthday parties, so I got it free.

That said, many of the most successful women interviewed for this book admitted – albeit briefly – to experiencing the odd pang of guilt, one of them recalling that when she read about Chelsea Clinton, suffering a mild injury in high school, telling the teachers that they should contact her father, because her mother was always busy, she remembered similar incidents and the slight shame she felt at the time.

> My partner was an artist who worked at home and was ecstatic at being mostly in charge of the children, but the story was passed around both our families and it was always recounted as a condemnation of me. I had to get over that – and my partner helped. He used to whistle the first few notes of the Piaf song *'Je Ne Regrette Rien'* and it always made me laugh.

Of course, every second chick-lit book on the tables at the airports carries a blurb saying 'Candi (or Cindi or Pippa) has it all…' What Candi, Cindi or Pippa have is children, a career, a great mate. Except – as the blurb writer tremblingly establishes – it really isn't possible to have it all, and Candi, Cindi or Pippa are just about to find: a) their partner is sleeping with their best friend; b) their seven-year-old has stabbed the family cat or; c) she's about to be passed over for promotion by someone she mentored and trusted.

The inescapable QED is that ambitious women who love their work can't also love their families. And that success involves some kind of surrender.

I don't accept that. Nor do most of the women I've talked to. This is the take of Síle McArdle, a lecturer and journalist.

> My definition of a successful working woman is one who has actively considered what's important

to her, and prioritised these needs and wants so that her work delivers it. If it's money, then, fine she's earning a decent amount. Or if it's working for a few hours out of the house but being available for school runs etc, then she's tracked down something flexible which allows for that. In other words, success isn't related to glass ceilings, killer heels, pinstripe suits or any of that guff about having to almost turn yourself into a man to 'succeed'. It's a true-to-yourself one where, every so often, the woman has taken a step back and said, 'What do I want?' – and, if necessary, recalibrated to make that happen, rather than just being swept along by: (a) what other people want; and (b) lack of focus because she doesn't know what she wants.

It's not a bad definition of success. But it does require hard work and ruthless clarity.

TEN THINGS SUCCESSFUL WORKING WOMEN WANT OTHER WOMEN TO KNOW:

1. If your job bores you, day in, day out, then neither money, status nor power will make that job enjoyable. Get out – even if it means taking a pay cut.
2. Don't blame your parents. In fact, don't blame anybody or anything for any downturns in your career or your happiness. Including yourself. Don't do the female guilt trip. Make your decisions and live with them without regrets. You're in charge of your own life. Make the best of it.
3. Never accept 'No' for an answer. Be pleasantly determined,

but if pleasant determination fails, use every system available to you, whether it's the appeals process when your job application gets rejected or the grievance system within your company.

4. Ask for help or advice. Not only do people love to give other people a leg-up, but it's a way of alerting, say, an executive in a different local authority or firm, or section within your own company to your potential

5. Become a great communicator. (And don't believe your own PR.)

6. Don't tell people about your failures, setbacks and disappointments. Sympathy disables.

7. Be constructively selfish. Take care of yourself.

8. Move on. If you discover you've done the wrong university course, shift to the right one. If you start in the wrong job, or even the wrong career, make a plan to get out of it by a set date and move relentlessly on that plan. You've only got one life. Most people, in their old age, regret more what they didn't do than what they did do.

9. Spend time with people you learn from.

10. Live in the present. Assuming that happiness will happen down the line is a bad idea. And don't postpone being good to other people until you become powerful or rich. Payback should be constant.

RESULTS OF *IMAGE* MAGAZINE BUSINESSWOMAN OF THE YEAR COMPETITION

Winner of Businesswoman of the Year 2008: Tanya Airey, Managing Director Sunway Travel.

Winners of Entrepreneur of the Year 2008: Rachael Doyle,

Arboretum Lifestyle and Garden Centre.
Winner of Young Businesswoman of the Year 2008: Emer Kennedy, Director of BT Ireland's Consumer South Division.
Winner of Professional Woman of the Year 2008: Jane Neill, Senior Executive in Davy Stockbrokers.

2

Don't Blame Your Parents

Shirley MacLaine once said of my father, Dean Martin: 'He was nice to everyone. He just didn't want nice to go on too long.'

But what can I say? He was my dad. I know he loved me. I just wish he'd been there more for me. I'd like to say I've moved on, but the feeling of loss still creeps back in. But I'm the only one in the family who ever stood up to him, and in the end I think I had the best of him. When he was ill I'd make him his grandmother's pasta fagioli. It was the only time in his life he asked me for anything. He'd call and say: 'Hi, baby. This is your dad.' Those words were musical to me.

People like him don't come along that often. What you saw was what you got.

Just don't make the mistake of asking for more.

Deana Martin, *Memories are Made of This* (Pan, 2008).

You can't pick your parents. It's so unfair. You get landed with these two strangers you'd never have selected, offered a choice. You didn't ask to be born to them. If you'd had a choice, you'd have wanted to be the daughter of a multi-billionaire. Or you'd have wanted to be the daughter of two people who didn't carry the trailing DNA wires of alcoholism, epilepsy or schizophrenia. Or you'd simply have wanted to be the daughter of a couple, rather than a single parent. Or you'd have wanted to be a boy.

Most of us went through that last stage, fighting for jeans rather than dresses, bored with dolls, hating the colour pink and reading about girls who got over their girlhood. Like Dora the Explorer or George in the Enid Blyton books. Some girls – a minority, but an ever-present minority – go through a phase of believing they were adopted, because they feel so unconnected to their parents.

We get over the phases of our childhood. But we never get over our childhood. Poet Philip Larkin summed up the general view:

> *They fuck you up, your Mum and Dad*
> *They do not mean to, but they do…*

But do they, really?

You're twenty now. Or thirty. Or older. Your life is OK but not great. Or maybe it's ropy as hell. In which case you go into therapy. Like one gorgeous woman I know who, like the blurbs on the back of the paperbacks always say 'has it all'. She's internationally famous, rich, owns a beautiful home wherein reside her gentle husband and her three daughters. She has more friends than she can cope with. She finds time to do charity work. But she also finds time to visit a therapist, because her days are threaded through with fear, self-contempt and a sense that a great black cloud is about to swamp her.

That black cloud is made up of a million tiny elements from her childhood and her teen years. The father who drank and disappeared. Constantly. The mother who placated and provoked him. The fear of flame that convinced her, every night, that her father's cigarette had set fire – again – to the couch and that the inferno was building, silently creeping the stairs towards her room. The dread of an invitation to stay the night at a friend's house, because of the impossibility of inviting the friend back to her house, where, even if her father was in one of his dry periods, she couldn't control the tendency of the budgie to use the 'c' word it had heard so often. The imperative to bring home good marks from school, while never letting on to the teachers that anything was wrong at home. Decent middle-class people kept their problems behind the double doors of the sun porch.

She thought she was free the day she walked into the dream job, the mermaid hair swinging, the grey eyes shining. Only to find, within weeks, that her looks turned the women against her and invited one of the men to assume she was easy. When she wasn't easy, he took her anyway, in the dark of an office after everybody else had gone home. It was her own fault, she figured, and the best thing to do was take the extra money and the promotion he put her way in order to protect himself.

Her looks became a weapon. Against herself. Since she mattered more because she was gorgeous, she had to stay gorgeous, and if that meant vomiting back up the full tub of Häagen-Dazs cookies-and-cream ice-cream, that's what she did, until her back teeth rotted and a doctor worked out the reasons why she had no periods and her face was hairy.

She's walking wounded but she's walking. And the one certainty she has is that she'll do better by her three little daughters than her parents did with her.

It's a kind of religion with her. Not an easy religion. Every day, her mother's axioms come, unbidden, into her head.

- 'Clean as you go, when you're making dinner.'
- 'Take that smirk off you, young woman.'
- 'They saw you coming. They always do.'
- 'Why can't you be like your sister? Your sister would never have done that.'
- 'What are you stuffing yourself with that rubbish for? You'll be the size of a house.'

She knows they were her mother's mad lassoing of reality in the hope of turning it into something better, of dragging it into her control. She knows they never worked for her mother, yet out they come in moments of stress, like when the youngest lies down on the floor in Tesco, screaming and drumming her heels in fury at a treat denied.

She does take some pride in limiting sweets without making a big issue out of it and of never commenting on the chubbiness of her eldest. That, too, is a reaction against her own poor rearing. She drives forward into motherhood, guided mainly by the rear-view mirror. Tiny, but ever-present in that rear-view mirror, is the reflection of the dysfunctional family that got her where she is today. Hers, she is resolved, will not be a dysfunctional family.

Fifteen years from now, her eldest daughter will blame her career/relationship/weight problems on the kind of upbringing she got. She will bitterly remember the warm positive suggestions that coiled around her teen years like a hungry cobra, choking the breath out of her with their unanswerable appropriateness. She will roll her eyes to heaven and do the 'I'm too busy for your idiotic chat' telephone snap when her mother rings her to find out how she's doing after the breakup with the boyfriend she'd thought was her mate for life.

In a fluctuating mess of uncertainties, one certitude will begin to build: when I have kids, I sure as hell won't bring them up the way I was brought up. My offspring will have a happy childhood.

It's the triumph of hope (and arrogance) over the sum total of human experience, this conviction that we can deliver a happy childhood to those to whom we give birth. It's linked to two other unquestioned certainties: that every child is entitled to a happy childhood; and that a happy childhood is the foundation for a productive and happy life. The first is a sweet – and essentially modern – aspiration. 'Childhood' as a separate and cherished period in life is only a couple of centuries old. Up to that point, children were put to work as soon as practicable, if they were of the working classes. If they were royalty, they were dressed as miniature adults and married off at nine or ten.

The idea that a happy childhood guarantees you a better later life is questionable. Among composers, for example, Mendelssohn is about the only one who had a joyous time as a child. The unhappier the childhood, for many artists and writers, the more driven the urge to create. Of course, the creation of a great work of art may give pleasure to others who later experience it, but deliver damn all happiness to its creator. That seems to have been the case with artists like Caravaggio, who may have created stunning beauty on canvas, but who were, as human beings, violent raping intemperate drunks.

Yet the belief is impregnable: of course someone who had a happy childhood is going to do well, later on. Except that it's only in the last sixty to seventy years that people have started to concentrate on trying to deliver the happy childhood to their offspring – and it's in precisely in the same time span that objectively-measured happiness levels have steadily declined.

It would be facile to suggest cause and effect but it would be equally facile not to point out that the sustained effort to improve the lives of children in the developed world has not produced generations of markedly happier adults.

One of the reasons may be that what we consciously do for our daughters may get unravelled, every day, by what we unconsciously do for them. A psychologist named Judith Langlois, who studied the interaction of new mothers with their babies, observed clear differences between the way mothers responded to pretty, as opposed to unattractive, newborn daughters:

> The less attractive the baby, the more the mother directed her attention to and interacted with people other than the baby. By three months...mothers of more attractive girls, relative to those with less attractive girls...more often kissed, cooed and smiled at their daughters while holding them close and cuddling them.

No doubt, if any of the mothers studied were to be asked about their interaction with their less attractive baby, they would instantly and fiercely deny that they engaged with the baby less warmly than if it had been beautiful. Of course they would. But what we believe we do and what we actually do aren't the same thing – and the less attractive baby girls were already getting a message hardwired into their brains about the need to be attractive.

And, according to Frank J. Sulloway, if the unfortunate girls were firstborns, they would probably feel responsible for not being pretty, too. Sulloway's massive *Born to Rebel*, published in the 1990s, looks at birth order and family dynamics. Its central thesis is that if you're born first in a family, you take on the position of the defender of the status quo, often identifying very closely with your parents. If you are laterborn, you are much more likely to be open, to be a speculative thinker, to be willing to take unorthodox theories on board:

> Most innovations in science, especially radical ones, have been initiated and championed by laterborns. Firstborns tend to reject new ideas, especially when the innovation appears to upset long-accepted principles. During the early stages of radical revolutions, laterborns are five to fourteen times more likely than firstborns to adopt the heterodox point of view. During technical revolutions, laterborns are two to three times more likely to lend their support. For their own part, firstborns are drawn to reactionary innovations, a domain in which they are also the principle pioneers. Firstborns typically welcome conservative doctrines as potential bulwarks against radical change, supporting them 2 to 1 over laterborns.

You'd get the impression from Sulloway that every woman who came first in her family is an ambitious, conservative control freak, while the youngest daughter is a lively, creative, adaptable and open-minded delight to have around. Like all generalisations, even evidenced generalisations, this one tends to get frayed at the edges when it moves from historical observation to one's own family experience. But the bottom line, whether we like it or not, is that where a girl happens in the line-up of a family influences what she grows up to be.

The next way that parents can screw up the lives of their children is by not getting along with each other. According to Professor Martin E.P. Seligman, divorce or fighting does not doom a child to years of unhappiness; it only makes it much more likely.

> Parents' fighting may hurt children in such a lasting way for one of two reasons. The first possibility is that parents who are unhappy with each other fight and separate. The fighting and separation directly disturb the child, causing long-term depression and pessimism. The second possibility is the traditional wisdom: fighting and separation themselves have little direct effect on the child, but awareness of parent's unhappiness is the culprit – so disturbing as to produce long-term depression. Only future research can clarify this, but although there is nothing in our data to tell us which of these two is right, I lean toward the first. I don't believe that children are subtle creatures with 'unhappiness in parents' detectors; in fact, I think that most children see their parents in a very positive light and that it takes real upheaval or deprivation to make a child notice how rotten things are.

Anthropologist Judith Rich Harris's study, *The Nurture Assumption* (Free Press, 1999), comes at this insight from a different angle, holding that parents, whether their own relationship is happy or unhappy, give themselves way too much credit and blame for how their kids turn out. Her thesis is that

DNA decides a chunk of it and peer influence decides the rest.

In the next chapter, we'll look at the influence of friends and schoolmates. In relation to genetics, however, we know that people have a greater tendency to get diabetes or asthma or psoriasis if these ailments run in their family.

Seligman and Rich Harris believe heritability goes further, saying that your personality as an adult is hugely influenced by genes, citing as evidence identical twins split at birth and reared in different families, far apart from each other, without any contact during their growing years. Compare those identical twins with fraternal – not identical twins – raised together, and the startling finding is that the identicals raised separately are more similar in adulthood than the fraternals raised together. They tend to share intelligence levels, have roughly the same sense of wellbeing or neuroticism and are alike in terms of authoritarianism, tendency to alcoholism and a rake of other traits. But you don't even have to go for the rare and interesting cases of identical twins to get the point: studies show that adopted children are much more like their biological parents (right down to having murderous tendencies or a liking for a particular brand of cigarette) than their adoptive parents.

All of which suggests that parents shape the lives of their children much less than popular myth and personal conviction would suggest. Nonsense, I hear you cry. I find myself every day getting more like my mother, whether I like it or not. Of course you do. You share the same genes. And to the women who might say, 'My mother gave me her values and I would have been a completely different person if I had been reared by someone else,' the answer is the same. Your mother passed on a goodly chunk of her DNA, transferring key aspects of her personality to you. You have a lot in common, under the skin. Some of your shared genes made you more likely to remember her values.

You want to believe she shaped you. (For the good, if you like her and like yourself. For the worst, if you think she did you life-long damage.) She probably wants to believe she shaped you, not least because the biographies of famous and successful people are replete with anecdotes of parents providing the turning point in their children's lives.

This tends to happen where a parent sees enormous potential within a child. It can be particularly effective not so much between mother and daughter as between father and daughter: a disproportionate number of successful businesswomen report being unusually close to their fathers and encouraged by them. Unfortunately, spotting the potential in a child sometimes sets parents awry, so that they create a constrained context of coercive ownership around a daughter (or a son) if they believe the girl (or boy) is exceptional and therefore shouldn't be subjected to the trauma of being surrounded by average kids.

While fostering your daughter's talent is important, whether that talent lies in athletics or archery, dance or music, and while it is also important to ensure that your daughter, if she is 'gifted' in the sense of having markedly and obviously higher IQ than her classmates, doesn't get bored by schooling she has already outpaced, profound danger to the happiness of a child lies in being pushed too hard. A friend of the parents of an African-American musical genius – Philippa Duke Schuyler – wrote a prescient letter of caution to them while the prodigy was still a little girl, a letter reproduced in Kathryn Talalay' s *Composition In Black and White: The Tragic Saga of Harlem's Biracial Prodigy* (Oxford, 1995):

> I am quite alarmed about the progress of your child. I would urge you to consult some educational experts before allowing her training to go further. The ones I have talked to agree that the premature development of the mind of one so young may in later years do harm to both mind and body…Also give her as much time as you can with other children. Too much adult society is not the best thing.

Of course they ignored him. They had on their hands a demonstrably gifted pianist and composer, whose mother regarded her daughter as a possession, an asset, whose public performances would fill the empty places in the mother's own life. The prodigy (like most prodigies) had a miserable life.

But before you start identifying with the rare cases of half-mad genius parents over-controlling the development of their genius child, consider how powerless that identification could make you. According to Martin E.P. Seligman:

> Seeing ourselves as victims of childhood makes us prisoners of the past and erodes our sense of responsibility. All successful therapy has two things in common: It is forward-looking and it requires assuming responsibility. Therapy that reviews childhood endlessly, that does not focus on how to cope in the here and now, that views a better future as incidental to undoing the past, has a century-long history of being ineffective. All therapy that works for depression, anxiety and sexual problems focuses on exactly what is going wrong now and on how to correct it. All this requires a heightened sense of

responsibility for our problems and a commitment to hard work (and even homework) to make the future better.

Good intentions are what the road to hell is paved with and the family is the transmission belt of pathology. Even today, when we're so educated about the ways to relate to our children, it's rare to hear a teenager say, 'My Mum's my best friend.' Or, 'My father is everything I want to be in life.'

Maybe we should lower our demands on ourselves as parents. Feed our children, clean them, hug them, listen to them, praise them and apologise in advance for the harm we don't know we're doing to them. Perhaps in a Larkin pastiche:

> *We do our best, us Mums and Dads.*
> *You may not think it, but we do…*

If you're too young to have kids of your own, but believe your Mum and Dad screwed you up, then you can waste a lot of time blaming them for it and picking at the scab.

Or you can let the scab fall off, cover up the scar and move into ownership of your own wonderful life.

> *You have brains in your head.*
> *You have feet in your shoes.*
> *You can steer yourself*
> *Any direction you choose.*
> *You're on your own. And you know what you know.*
> *And YOU are the guy who'll decide where to go.*
>
> Dr Seuss, The Places You'll Go

3

Don't Blame the Nuns

*I wanted to be a nun. I saw nuns as superstars. When
I was growing up, I went to a Catholic school, and
the nuns, to me, were these superhuman, beautiful,
fantastic people...*

Madonna

Parents are bad enough but no matter how rotten they are, at
least they're of your blood. (Not that this is of much consolation
if they're spilling some of what is supposed to stay inside you.)

Some unlucky women are brought up in orphanages. Television programmes over the past twenty years have brought
home, in living colour and dramatic recreation, the lives of
children in some of the orphanages and other institutions – like
reform schools – run by religious. The state, in the person of
Bertie Ahern, then Taoiseach, has apologised to those who, often
because of family poverty or other circumstances, were torn from
their homes and relatives and subjected to a brutally regulated
regime. Some of the children, particularly those sent to reform
schools, most of them for offences which would be regarded as
minor today, were starved, beaten and ritually humiliated. Some
of them were sexually abused by those set to care for them.

The line of culpability for what happened to generations of

little girls and boys runs right through society, much as we would like to load it all on to the religious who were at the sharp edge of it. Ireland was poor and harsh during the 1930s and 1940s, and if you were a child living with your family on a poor farm in, say, the west of Ireland, your quality of life was not what would be considered minimally acceptable today.

The state incorporated lofty thoughts about the centrality of cherished children in a free Ireland into the 1937 Constitution and then didn't give the religious orders enough money to properly provide for the ones the state delivered into their care. Nor did it create a system of monitoring the way childcare was delivered which would actually ensure any standards were met.

And then there were the nuns and brothers, saintly in aspiration, who were responsible, all day every day, for the rearing of hundreds of children disadvantaged by circumstance. We know the stories of vicious Christian Brothers and of nuns who forced pre-teens to work in chilblained misery like characters in a Dickens novel.

We know how powerful those black-gowned nuns must have seemed to the little ones – and to the rest of Ireland. Because the nuns and brothers and priests were everywhere. Every family photograph from the 1930s, 1940s or 1950s, whether it's of a wedding or a wedding anniversary or a christening, features at least one black-garbed religious. Today, such photographs don't carry that dark-suited character at all. Arguably the most radical change in a twentieth century awash in profound societal change was the destruction of the population in monasteries and convents. A virus could not have depopulated those institutions more effectively. Those inside left. Those outside stopped coming in. A few in each institution held on in isolation, to create structures they hoped would pass on to lay people the key elements of an ethos they had loved.

Nobody celebrated the contribution to modern Ireland of the nuns and brothers and priests. In the TV programmes surrounding the millennium, they were visually present, but no more than that. It wasn't safe, at that point, to even talk mildly positively about religious. You could get painted into a corner as approving of child abuse or as a reactionary right-winger.

Which is a pity, for two reasons. From a woman's point of view, it wipes out of history some of the most influential women who have ever lived and worked in Ireland, any one of whom left more of a real mark on posterity than did, for example, the ludicrously over-hyped Countess Markiewicz. But the abandonment of attention to this important aspect of our collective history also means that we fail to ask the questions: why did so many men and women enter religious life in the late nineteenth and early twentieth centuries and was it a good thing?

The men who became priests and brothers can be dealt with by others. The women joined because of choice and lack of choice. Post-Famine Ireland was – in the main – a dire and dismal place in which to be a woman. You grew up illiterate, because any money for education went to improve the chances of the boys in the family. You worked from the time you were mobile. You married young, if at all. You had as many children as God sent you, grieving through the horrific deaths of the babies taken by diphtheria, the removal of pre-teens who suffered polio and were consigned to specialist institutions, the withering away of teenagers who contracted 'galloping consumption' or TB. (The mother of one Minister for Health in living memory, Dr John O'Connell, could neither read nor write and saw two of her children die of tuberculosis in their teens.)

Against that background, entering a convent held enormous

promise. For the poor and uneducated, that promise was not total. If you entered a religious order without a dowry, you tended to stay at the lower level within that order as an unpaid cook or cleaner. But, even then, marriage to Christ must have seemed a better option than marriage to some old man picked by your parents.

For bright ambitious girls from homes that could scrape together a dowry, the convent offered a career no other area of Irish life offered at that time. Some of the women who created religious orders or who joined established orders achieved a level of power equivalent to the contemporary power wielded by a Mary Harney, a Danuta Gray or a Gillian Bowler. They oversaw huge projects, managed – for the time – vast budgets, deployed thousands of staff and created institutions which have lasted to this day. They changed the physical and social landscape of their nation.

Sometimes, they changed those landscapes in Ireland, having come from other countries. Like the group of young women who set up a religious order dedicated to giving good care (or '*bon secours*') to poor Parisians. Catherine O'Farrell, an Irishwoman living in Paris at the time, persuaded four of them to come to Ireland in 1861, to care for the sick and dying in their homes. Later, they began to set up hospitals, together with nursing homes for elderly patients. Today, the Bon Secours health system is the biggest provider of private health care in Ireland.

Paris also played a part in the life-story of Nano Nagle, who, a couple of years back, was the unexpected winner of RTÉ's Ireland's Greatest Women contest. Educated in Paris when the Penal Laws prohibited Catholic education in Ireland, Nagle chose religious life rather than the comfortable marriage her dowry would have entitled her to. Not only did she have an unprecedented vision of a nationwide system of education for women, she had the determination and competence to make it happen. Simultaneously devout and lawless, she was a relentless genius at getting recognition, permission and money out of the establishment.

No woman in modern times matches what Nano Nagle of the Presentation and other order-founders like Catherine McAuley of the Mercy order achieved: long before feminism, these women set up education (for girls) and health care (for everybody) when all the odds were stacked against them. They submerged their sexual and maternal yearnings for the common good.

The legislative milestones on the road to the emancipation of women in Ireland and to their validation as equal citizens are easy to identify. The names of feminists who fought for gender-equality during the 1960s and 1970s are less easy to recall. And the foundation for the achievement of these fundamental freedoms is rarely acknowledged. That foundation was laid by religious orders such as the Mercy and Presentation sisters, who were central to the movement of the majority of women in Ireland away from subservient illiteracy. The sisters created a context of entitlement and expectation for girls which had never previously existed. Their pupils learned much more than an academic curriculum. The gains from team sports provided a subtle balance to the gains delivered by individual classes in music and other specialisms.

The foundation of each order's education infrastructure was a magnificent undertaking, particularly when understood against the economic and attitudinal background of the times. The continuum, however, is arguably just as exceptional. A glance at newspapers through the decades establishes that most businesses set up contemporaneously with the foundation of the congregations and the setting up of their schools have either disappeared or have been submerged through takeovers. Yet the congregations committed to education for women grew and adapted to changes which sank many commercial entities.

As a result, the schools they ran became a central assumption in Irish family life. These days, that central assumption tends to manifest itself only when challenged: parents are outraged by the possibility of the closure or sale of a school attended by several generations of the same family. They see such a possibility as the sundering of what might be called a 'contract of conviction'. This unwritten contract between the congregation, with its schools, traditions and values on the one hand, and the community on the other, is an essential, if largely unexamined, strand in Irish life.

That said, it is inarguable that some of the students who passed through convent schools and many of those who passed through religious-run orphanages, suffered greatly during their time 'with the nuns'. The misery of those who went through orphanages has been acknowledged by the state, which has provided some financial compensation, together with the opportunity for those who see themselves as victims of those institutions to tell their story and put on the record precisely how they were treated and the pain it caused them.

However, any woman who feels she was damaged by her upbringing should not buy into the belief that she is permanently and irrevocably crippled as a result. International research establishes that the impact of horrible events in childhood is not insurmountable.

For example, an Australian researcher named David Maunders found and interviewed grown-ups who remembered their childhood years in orphanages in Australia, the US and Canada.

What distinguished the adults with whom he talked was that they had not been born in the orphanages. They had been delivered to the institutions when they were four or five, and so could remember their own incarceration. (And that's how many of them recalled it.) Remember, these were children at the age at which Irish children now go to primary school. They do so, most of them, having spent time in play groups or nursery schools, so the trauma is lessened. Yet mothers and fathers worry about how lonely and frightened their child may be, facing into Junior Infants.

The children Manders studied, in sharp contrast, were moving away from their families completely. They had no hope of returning home at the end of the day, to be comforted over whatever had gone wrong during that day. They worked from morning to night, scrubbing, cleaning, preparing food, going to the schoolroom. They were often cold and hungry. One of them told the researcher how she kept herself alive:

> I can remember going to bed every night and thinking 'When I wake up this dream will be over.' And I would wake up and it wasn't. But I would do that every single night that I lived there.

It's an infinitely sad piece of research. But an infinitely hopeful one, also. Because the orphanage-reared adults, despite the poverty, deprivation and in some cases overt cruelty of their childhood years, went on to live effective lives, marrying, having children and developing careers.

It's not the only pointer to the survival capacities of children. Thousands of children who survived the concentration camps of the Nazi era in Germany, Poland and elsewhere went on to educate themselves, marry, raise children and contribute to society in whichever country they lived, after the second world war.

That's the good news. Circumstances can be pushed to one side by a determined teenager moving into adulthood, and a good life achieved.

4

Don't Blame Your Peers – or Be Led by Them

There's one advantage to being 102. There's no peer pressure.

Dennis Wolfberg

The bottom line is that peers, much more than parents or teachers, are the most important influences on a child's life as they progress into the teen years.

Within months of their birth, many babies are among others of their own age in crèches. Within a couple of years of their birth, the overwhelming majority are in nursery schools, play groups or kindergartens, learning about sharing with others and observed by experts in childcare who speedily notice if little Jessica goes over to a corner, eschewing the company of her peers and who draw this to the attention of little Jessica's mother. It is rarely reported to Jessica's Ma as an indicator of future greatness. Au contraire, it's usually seen as a problem. We have moved towards the Eastern view of socialisation, preferring the group to the individual and believing that it is through service to the group that the individual becomes fully human.

We may be correct in this move, although almost every great

shift in the rules around child-development has subsequently had its teeth kicked in by later theory. Even if correct, though, this early socialising comes at a cost. At more than one cost. The first negative consequence is where the innately human wish to belong gets turned into an overriding daily imperative. Even the FedEx man played by Tom Hanks in the movie about a character lost on a desert island expresses this need: he develops an extraordinarily close relationship with a basketball. (Of course, many women in Ireland would claim that it didn't take being marooned on an island to make their boyfriends develop a weirdly close relationship with a football and those who play with it.)

The second consequence (which is anything but negative for manufacturers of products aimed at teenagers) is that, whereas teenagers, in the relatively recent past, were the age-group feeling the pressure to own a particular brand of shoe or have a specific piece of jewellery, lest they feel 'uncool' and excluded from their peer group, now they need to demonstrate membership of a desired group much earlier. Pre-teens are devastated by the prospect of wearing a brand of jeans they believe will mark them as much as the bell carried by lepers in Biblical times that sent out the message 'Unclean! Unclean!'

Just over ten years ago, an American advertising agency set out to study what they called the 'global teen demographic', looking at the day-to-day behaviours and choices of teenagers. The study specifically looked at young people between fifteen and eighteen across forty-five countries.

'Despite different cultures, middle-class youth all over the world seem to live their lives as if in a parallel universe,' observed the final report. 'They get up in the morning, put on their Levis and Nikes, grab their caps, backpacks and Sony personal CD players, and head for school.'

It makes for a wonderful marketing opportunity. And it makes for a problem called 'peer pressure'.

One of the funniest examples of peer pressure in action was recorded for television long before teenagerdom had ever been defined or exploited. An American producer of Candid Camera set up the elevator in a sky-scraping office block, so that the planted passengers all face the wrong way.

Think about it. The lift doors open, and if it's already occupied, you, the new passenger, find yourself facing the occupants, because, in one of these conveyances (the safest methods of transport in the world, by the way) everybody faces the door.

In this filmed instance, however, everybody didn't face the door. As soon as it opened, new arrivals found themselves looking at an array of backs. They got into the lift, and what happened next was the interesting thing. At first, they faced the door. The camera caught their facial expressions, which started at certainty, moved into doubt and ended up at worried. Sooner or later, all the newcomers to the lift caved in and joined the others facing the back wall of the elevator. Now, this wasn't a modern elevator with two working doors, one back and one front. It had just one exit. Logically, therefore, any sentient occupant knew that if he or she wanted to get out of the lift, they should face the door. Yet, because the majority of people were facing the back wall, even though nobody said a word to them, the rest joined the illogical consensus of a group who were their peers for only a few minutes and presented their back view to the exit.

Peer pressure is felt by every age group, and those who most passionately deny that they are subject to it tend to be the most obvious victims of it. Although 'victim' may be too pejorative a word. Sir Robert Baden-Powell tapped into the positive aspects of peer pressure when he created the Boy Scout movement, which in turn gave birth to the Girl Guides. Based on the collective responsibility carried by soldiers in wartime, where a fighter is expected to and expects to support and protect his colleagues, these movements created a positive sense of community and of community responsibility among generations of children.

Today, mobile phones provide the connectedness among teens and pre-teens, as do social networking web sites like Bebo and My Space. What they don't generate, of course, is a sense of community responsibility. Electronic networking tends to be a clustering of the 'cool' as they share their accounts of the latest drinking bout and a fierce exclusion of the 'uncool' as individuals are picked on, excluded, bullied and made to look and feel ridiculous, to such an extent that for some of them, suicide is the only way out.

Women in their twenties recall the absolute requirements of acceptance by their peer group: the running shoes which were acceptable and the running shoes that marked you as a dork The pastimes that mattered and the ones that didn't. It was of no moment, for example, that the massed forces, medical and parental, of the adult world told you smoking cigarettes might kill you. That possibility was too far in the future to matter, whereas the entrée to the desired group offered by smoking was an immediate and potent reward.

Part of peer pressure in adolescence is the consensus around the concept that one's parents are complete morons. It's not total, that pressure. One sixteen-year-old, asked to write anonymously for this book, talks of 'having a good thing going on' with her parents and claims to be resistant to peer pressure:

Today I started thinking about my career. Well, correction, not specifically my career but what course I want to take in college. This was probably not the best of ideas.

I am sixteen years old and what bothers me? Peer pressure? Nope. I am probably the most stubborn person this side of the Atlantic. I relish the feeling that I have done the complete opposite to what someone has told me to do. School work? Maybe for about one minute and then I get distracted by shoes or a movie or gossip. The economic state of the country? Hmm…not likely.

The thing that really worries me, keeps me up at night, makes me quiet and serious at random intervals during the day and seems to be hanging over my head constantly, threatening to explode, is the question of what I'm going to study at college.

Let me just give you a tour of what went through my mind as I flicked through the Trinity College prospectus some evil person had left on the kitchen table.

One minute in: 'God, maybe medicine isn't such a good idea after all…OK, next option.'

Three minutes in: 'Psychology might be good but I'd feel like a total hypocrite telling people to 'open up' to me when I turn into Frosty the Snowman every time someone wants to know about my feelings.

Five minutes in: 'English literature may be good…Oh no, wait. They talk about sexualities. Seeing as I have the sense of humour of a thirteen-year-old boy that might not be too good.'

Seven minutes in: 'I wish I was Paris Hilton! She does absolutely nada and gets millions for it!'

After this I retired to an empty room with my i-Pod until I could function normally again and had stopped breathing like an asthmatic in a sawdust factory.

This whole episode got me thinking about how people blame their problems on their childhood. (I never said I was particularly logical. Don't ask, OK, just bear with me.)

When you're a child, all you want to be is older. Then when you're my age, you're worried about what will happen when you are older. So now you're telling me that when I am older I am going to be worrying about the fact that my childhood has ruined me and given me a thousand different hang-ups?

Wait, wait, wait. When do I get to enjoy things? When can I just sit back and relax?

Being a teenager, I was suddenly filled with resentment (this is, after all, apparently what we do best). I started to resent the people who are blaming all their problems on childhood. What happened in the past happened. That's it. Non-changeable, not-returnable. It's set. My future can go a hundred million different ways. I have no idea what's going to happen. It's scary and it's crazy and it's great! My future is an open book. The childhood people are blaming their problems on? That's closed.

I don't know what's going to happen to me in the future. I might be a doctor, or a teacher or Paris Hilton's best buddy (fingers crossed!). But I do know that I'm not going to let something that happened when I was five or ten or fifteen ruin it for me. It's the only thing (I think) I know for sure.

Nevertheless, for most teenage girls, their parents are an ever-present reality whose approval is not as important as the approbation of their peers, and who, too often, are determined to limit the freedom which every other girl in the class seems to have.

One teenager says:

> The absolute confession of failure, when I was fifteen, was to know what had been on *The Late Late Show* on Friday night. I remember sitting, crying on the couch, watching the programme because my Mam wouldn't let me go to Wesley, and knowing that on Monday, when everybody else would be comparing notes about what had happened to who, I'd be silent, letting on not to care, but of course I cared.

It's impossible to persuade a teenager that the approval of her classmates, especially those among her classmates who belong to the Alpha group of attractive, successful and cool kids, will not matter a jot in years to come. The need, at the time, is too overwhelming. It is impossible to shake the conviction held by a teenager that the whispered snide remark she half-hears, followed by harsh group laughter at her expense, will not matter to her, down the line. The pain, at the moment it happens, is too acute.

There's no comforting you, if you're somewhere in your teens and feel you're a fat spotty moron who is so uncool you should almost be put in the brown bin and carted off for composting. You know the truth inside yourself. You know your life won't be improved by drinking cider in a field with damp seeping into the backside of your jeans, when you'd prefer Cidona anyway. But you'll do it because it's a laugh. Not much of a laugh. But better than loneliness and rejection.

There's no point in anybody older than you telling you that some day you're going to look at the photographs of this period in your life and realise you weren't ugly. That, in fact, you had a lot going for you, in the looks department. The future isn't relevant to you. It's all about today, tomorrow, the coming weekend.

There's no point in someone pointing out to you – as, throughout your life, people will idiotically point out to you – that you're not alone. Neither were those who drowned on the *Titanic*. Didn't make going under for the third time fun. Misery loves company, yes. But it wants the company that's most likely to exclude it. It wants the company of shiny happy people from whom it can draw warmth and support. Shag the notion that putting misery with other miserable people will somehow make things easier. It won't.

Of course it's possible that you'll come across a poem or a song that reaches out over time and distance to crystallise the experience you're going through. Janis Ian's 'At Seventeen' has offered that experience to countless women, who know they've done what the singer confesses: 'inventing lovers on the phone'. I did it, as a teenager. I told my friend Anne Sheehy the most Godawful lies about a boyfriend I didn't have.

He lived in England, but was in constant contact with me. Bought me wonderful presents (which, of course, I beggared myself to buy, including a gold ring I bought in a street I'd never shopping in before – Aungier Street – for fear anybody I knew would catch me at it.)

My imaginary boyfriend taught me fiction-writing. I had to note down his birthday, his middle name, his breakfast preferences. I had to study the history of the town he didn't live in and the profession the father he didn't have didn't have. If you follow me. Fortunately, I killed off his mother early on, so I didn't have to craft a bloody biography for her and learn it.

Did Anne believe me? I don't know. I've never asked her. (She was my bridesmaid when I married a real guy, a few years later.) I've never confessed until now. Because now, I'm at a safe distance from my teens. Thanks be to Jasus. I'd rather be dead than go back to them.

If you're having the teen years from hell, here's a truth nobody tells you at the time. Your parents complain about all the hassles in their lives, but nothing, *nothing*, is as bad as being the teenager who is left out and who is secretly convinced that the others are right to leave her out. No matter how tough phases of the rest of your life are, they'll never be as bad as now. Never.

You don't believe me, I know. You need a lifeline, and a promise from some old fart isn't it.

Well, here's a proven lifeline. Write it down. Keep a diary. Somewhere nobody else can find it. Don't show it to anybody. Just write down the worst of what happens to you and the worst that you do – because you will do strange and shaming things during these years. Keep a record. It will be the beginning of survival. Humankind tells itself stories to understand the world around it and one of the great stories, different for every single individual, is the story of the rite of passage into adulthood. Unfortunately, those stories rarely get told, as A.N. Wilson pointed out when he wrote that:

> The vast majority of the human race drifts without record from conception to extinction. Their lives go unrecorded, and it is only theology which might make us suppose that these individual lives have any previous or future existence, or indeed during their palpable existence on earth, that they have any identifiable existence. For most, it is a tale full of sound and fury signifying nothing, but the most significant of all, it is a tale that is not told.

Write down what happens to you.

Do not live an unrecorded life. Who knows? You might even get a novel out of it later.

Much later.

5

Exams and Qualifications

Credentialism – tying good jobs to diplomas – made a university degree into a meal ticket.
Charles Derber, William A. Schwartz, Yale Magrass,
Power in the Highest Degree (Oxford, 1990).

Every year, around about April, we start to head into an annual whinge-fest about the awful challenge posed to delicate students by the Leaving and Junior Certificate exams.

Women with kind voices on radio programmes explain how not to get stressed out over the prospect of being asked to prove that the student has actually learned something in their years in secondary school. Newspaper columns tell students to take a break every hour or so and do stretching exercises. Anguished mothers claim that an exam is unfair on the sensitive student who may lose a marble or two under pressure and fail to do themselves justice.

Now, secondary school students deserve sympathy. School, while improved in recent decades, is still tough. Still filled with covert competition, with smart-arse snideries, with constant regulation. No matter how awful the later happenings in a business career, they're usually minor-league compared to the way school can tattoo inadequacy and exclusion on the soul of the student. The point is that exams are the escape route from this problem, not the problem itself. The recurring notion that a teacher's assessment should count for marks in exams is well-intended nonsense. Most of us believe everybody else to be biased, bigoted and generally lacking in the insight to fully appreciate wonderful *us*, whereas we credit ourselves with impartiality, generosity of observation and Oscar-winning insight. It's one of those self-deceptions without which life would be unliveable.

But to assume for a moment that teachers are in some way gifted with the unique capacity to put their own gut reactions to one side, to ignore their deep-rooted loathing of that kid in the corner with the supercilious smirk on him and the father who is obnoxious whenever he comes near the school in his bull-barred SUV and give the student a scrupulously impartial assessment is to assume teachers get sainthood along with their qualifications.

They don't. They just don't. One of my teachers hated me with a passion admirable in one so small. It started when, as sports mistress, she ordered me to try out camogie. I watched an experienced group of players do a manoeuvre, the culmination of which was a sweeping stroke by one of them which removed the front teeth of another in a flying spray of white fragments and aspirated blood. I handed the under-sized nun my stick, took the injured girl to hospital and refused to have anything more to do with camogie, thereby marking myself as unpatriotic, disloyal to the school, a wimp and a slob. It's always good to know where you stand.

Now, imagine if that particular teacher had the capacity to provide or withhold marks in the Leaving Cert in relation to me. I'd have been down the educational tubes, without a point to my name. Because the exam was an objective test marked by total strangers, however, I was home free.

In advance of any objective test, it's inevitable that a student or trainee will be nervous. Inevitable – and right and proper. It's also inevitable that nervousness will cause some students or trainees to perform markedly poorer than might otherwise have been expected. (Although not half as many as claim to have been done in by terror. It's an excuse that covers a multitude.)

But the reality is that many of the careers students aim at require the capacity to muster data and judgment under pressure. If, for example, a potential pilot who was a likeable and diligent student throughout their school life loses their capacity to think and access their own knowledge under the pressure of an examination hall, they're sure as shootin' not going to be the pilot you want in charge of your next flight. The Leaving and Junior Certs should serve not just as a way of measuring capacity to learn but of capacity to perform under pressure.

That said, one has to raise questions about the largely artificial pressure exerted by the 'mock' Junior and Leaving Cert which come round after Christmas in most schools. The problem with them is that they are now the first real step towards the 'credentialism' that grips Irish society. You can be clever, resourceful, a lateral thinker, creative and experienced, but if you don't have a degree, the computer systems in the companies to which you apply are likely to disqualify you at source, never allowing you to get near an interview.

That puts chills up my uncredentialled spine, because I have no degree. I have a diploma in elocution but that's not exactly cap-and-gown stuff. Because I am so mortified by my lack of degrees, my family has rallied around in their unique ways. My husband suggests that marriage should allow a shared weight and a shared set of degrees. This would be mighty, because he's phenomenally thin and has half a dozen degrees, albeit in subjects of minimal commercial value, like Classics and Theology.

My son, who is now my boss, takes a rather more brutal approach. Have a look at the web site of the company where I work, www.communicationsclinic.ie and view my biography. He wrote it.

I did go to university. That makes it worse, not better. I worked incredibly hard in school and got an impressive Leaving Cert, which nobody has ever asked to look at. Not that I carry it around in my briefcase or anything, but it would have been pleasant to produce it to general acclaim. So I took my Leaving Cert and went to UCD and within weeks was floundering. I chose to read Philosophy and English. Philosophy, it was clear after a fortnight, was way beyond the capacity of my few brain cells.

Then the Abbey actress Joan O'Hara got pregnant. As a result, she could not take part in the production of Boucicault's *The Shaughraun* in the Aldwych Theatre, London. At the time, I was a member of the Abbey's repertory company and a brilliant mimic. I could act and sing the part in blatant imitation of Joan's performance. I was offered the job, knowing – sad, sad – that it would mean pulling out of first year in college. The relief was stupendous. The guilt, equally so. To this day (or rather, night) I have nightmares about the exam I never sat.

Gillian Bowler, the woman who turned Budget Travel into a multimillion Euro business and who's chaired Fáilte Ireland and Irish Life and Permanent, has no such nightmares, although she dropped out of formal education even earlier than I did.

'I had really liked school when I was there,' she remembers. 'I thought politics, philosophy and economics at the London School of Economics sounded trendy and I would have been interested in those subjects.' By way of preparation, she did an entrance exam – at fourteen – at a local college where the majority of the students were eighteen. 'I got through and I did that for a year.' But then the call of swinging London caused her to toss academia and set up, all on her own, in that city when she was fifteen and a half. The rest is commercial history.

Gill Bowler found that cop-on and curiosity served her better than a degree. I found the same. I also got lucky. I had friends and colleagues who wanted work done by someone who could do it, rather than by someone who had a degree. Because, as the years passed, a degree replaced the Leaving Cert as a basic qualification for any worthwhile job, and autodidacts like me found themselves unqualified for jobs they could do with their hands tied behind their backs. Credentialism took over. As the authors of *Power in the Highest Degree*, quoted at the beginning of this chapter, say, the move has major negative implications:

> Credentialling denies those who have acquired knowledge outside of professional institutions the right to compete in the job market and demonstrate their own expertise. A self-taught psychologist with a large body of published work but without a PhD is unlikely to become a Professor of Psychology, despite the occasional uncredentialled luminary like Erik Erikson.

Not that this is new. In Imperial China, the level of education and knowledge possessed by the mandarins separated them – to their advantage – from the uneducated minority.

In medieval Europe, learning and skills were so precious that they were guarded by specific ordinances. Like the one articulated by a tailor's guild in the early sixteen hundreds:

> No person of this fraternity from henceforth shall discover or disclose any of the lawful secrets concerning the feats of merchandising in their own occupation or any secret counsel of the said fraternity which ought of reason and conscience to be secretly kept without an utterance thereof to any other person of another mystery.

Accredited third-level learning is no longer guarded by such strictures, but it does provide access to careers and jobs less qualified people can't hope for. Which brings us to the classic question: but are they happy, having attained their degrees?

The short answer is: not necessarily. When Ireland's economy took a turn for the worse, earlier this year, the government took action. It announced a public service job freeze. Within weeks, phone-in programmes were taking calls from embittered new graduates who were qualified and eager to take up much-needed jobs in, say, social work, but who, because of the freeze, knew they would have to emigrate.

Around the same time, Minister Mary Hanafin indicated that social welfare payments to the unemployed would have a new wrinkle, as far as the jobless young were concerned. They would be encouraged to go back into education. Cynics would suggest that, while taking them off the live register, this had the dubious benefit of getting them ever more qualifications which would over-qualify them for the jobs they still couldn't get.

Of course, time spent reading and researching is intrinsically rewarding. However, it carries a downside of its own. In recent years, my company, which prepares people for job interviews (see the next chapter) has identified a negative trend for the hyper-qualified, best summed up, off-the-record, by one human resources manager. She said:

> In theory, when someone pitches up in front of me with two Masters degrees, I should be ecstatic. Except what I'm looking at is someone in their late twenties who's spent a decade in academia. They've no work experience, except maybe bar-tending in Australia. They've no real life experience of solving problems, motivating people nor coping with crises. Analysing case studies in college may give them greater wisdom. What I need is energy, a bit of knowledge, but above all the capacity to get along with other people and show a bit of cop-on. I don't often see the last two in the multi-Masters graduates.

The real difficulty is where the narrowing of options, often done with the well-meaning help of parents and the apparently expert help of career-guidance teachers, winds up putting the highly qualified graduate in a job they truly hate. It can happen to a bishop. (And has.) Or to a genius.

> If I would be a young man again and had to decide how to make my living, I would not try to become a scientist or a scholar or teacher. I would rather choose to be a plumber or a peddler in the hope to find that modest degree of independence still available under present circumstances.

That's what Einstein said, looking back on his career. He

was subject to a contextual reality that no longer obtains. Or – to put it more simply – everybody's got more options, these days. You can get a degree in law and then shift into medicine. You can get no degree at all, wander the world, try out various businesses and then become a mature third-level student. You can study accountancy and get practical experience – at home or internationally – while you do it in a company like KPMG.

Just make up your mind. And don't buy any myths. If you want to get a degree in civil engineering, pharmacy, medicine or law, you will end up with a qualification which will allow you to do things. If you want to get a degree in English (which started as a placebo for women students who were considered incapable of scientific disciplines) or Philosophy, don't kid yourself that you know how to do anything. You may have a great time in college. You may have a social life that belongs in the *Guinness Book of Records*. All that is good. But for career-building, a few years' experience, even offered for free to a good company, can be a better launch pad.

Either come out with something you can do, or get a job. Or admit it's a three-year holiday.

And when you go for a job interview (having obeyed the instructions in the next chapter) regard the degree on your CV as a paper qualification, after which it's up to you to prove you have the competences to make you employable.

6

Acing the Job Interview

First of all, I look for their level of energy. Next comes competence. Are they prone to making mistakes? Have they been making major or minor mistakes? Can they recover from those mistakes? Everyone is entitled to make mistakes, but you want people who make recoverable mistakes. Can you learn from them or are they very destructive? Then comes brainpower. A lot of times, you hire someone who you think is very smart, and then you learn that person isn't very smart at all. Energy level, drive, competence and brainpower.

Donald Trump

The first thing to realise, when you go for a job interview, especially the one which will allow you to set your foot on the first step of the career ladder, is that it's not all about you. It may feel as if it's all about you. But it's not.

It's all about the needs of the company or organisation to which you've applied.

No. Don't skip that sentence as if it was obvious. Read it again. Learn it off by heart. Apply it. Apply it, not just when you get in front of the HR manager or panel of interviewers, but in advance, when you're researching what you're going to offer.

For years, when I've prepared women for job interviews, I've been struck by the self-directedness of their thinking. Here's a small sample of comments made:

- I want to work with your company because I would be able to cycle to the plant.
- Appointment to this post would give me a great start on my five-year career plan.
- I'm the sort of person who likes to work at home so I'd like to talk to you about that.
- I'm good at working with people and I'd prefer a position where I worked within a team.
- I wouldn't want to spend a lot of time in manufacturing but experience in a company like this would be a start.

All these remarks refer to the applicant's needs, not the needs of the potential employer. Why should the employer want to contribute to a great start in an applicant's five-year plan, which is likely to take them somewhere other than their 'starter' company?

None of the remarks reveal interest in, knowledge of, or insight into, the particular company the applicants had applied to. They don't even name the company.

A potential employer who knows how to do a good recruitment interview will spot and disqualify a self-directed employee within minutes of the start of the interview. The fact that this dismissal doesn't happen more often is partly due to the unwarranted confidence many recruiters have in their own intuition. They set out in an unstructured way to interview a candidate, certain that they'll spot the characteristics the company needs, positive that they will identify the traits of the right person, convinced that they will know and like the right person by the end of a casual chat.

It's a bit like a first date – and has roughly the same percentage of good results. On early dates in male-female relationships, according to two Canadian psychologists who researched the area, young people ignore facts that don't fit with the impression they form. They decide the other person is generous, witty, compassionate and talented. Their friends and relations, watching the early stages of the relationship, decide the other person is mean, dull, self-absorbed and thick as two short planks.

And you know what? The friends and relations are usually right. The person in the relationship makes excuses:

- 'Oh, he let me pick up that bill because he knows I don't like women who freeload.'
- 'He was just so tired that night, he wasn't himself.'
- 'No, you don't realise, he would have taken me to the hospital that night I broke my ankle, he just didn't realise it was a fracture.'
- 'He left that company because they just didn't seem to cop on to his being way better than any of the other people in that department.'

Precisely the same thing happens, according to Professor Allen Huffcutt of Bradley University in the United States, in a huge proportion of recruitment interviews. Managers develop an impression of a particular candidate and ditch at source any objective data which would prove that impression wrong.

Interviewed by the brothers Brafman for their delightful book, *Sway*, Huffcutt produced a list of the most commonly asked questions in recruitment interviews:

1. Why should I hire you?
2. What do you see yourself doing five years from now?
3. What do you consider to be your greatest strengths and weaknesses?
4. How would you describe yourself?
5. What college subject did you like the best and the least?
6. What do you know about our company?
7. Why did you decide to seek a job with our company?
8. Why did you leave your last job?
9. What do you want to earn five years from now?
10. What do you really want to do in life?

Huffcutt rightly regards all but one of these questions as a waste of air – as an example of 'first date' interrogation. He makes an exception of question 6.

The invitation to self-description in the fourth question, for instance, simply offers the opportunity for the candidate to spiel off prepared guff about being hardworking, committed, energetic, a good team player, just as that other useless question, 'What is your greatest weakness?' nearly always evokes a rueful admission that the candidate is a perfectionist. Well, shucks. That's a weakness?

I did once, a long time ago, interview a psychiatrist in preparation for his going for a consultancy post in a big acute hospital. I threw the weakness question because I figured it was likely to happen in the real interrogation.

'Procrastination,' he responded.

'Mmm?'

'Postponement. Not meeting deadlines. Putting off to

tomorrow what I should do today.'

He was on a roll. All I had to do was nod encouragingly to get more than ten straight minutes of a confession to complete incompetence and an obsessive reluctance to meet any potential employer's time lines. You'd be absolutely sure, having listened to him, that he had arranged to be born two weeks beyond his due date and would have stayed in the womb forever, had that been a real option.

Most people are not quite so unemployably honest as this psychiatrist and as a result, the question is rarely worth asking.

The only question in the list given earlier rated as worthwhile by the professor who has spent two decades studying the outcomes of job interviews is Number 6: What do you know about our company?

'That can actually be a decent question,' Huffcutt says. 'It gets into whether they took the time to research your company, which can be a good sign.'

Taking the time to research the company to which you're applying is a vital step before you do an interview. It gives you a port to go to. (It may, on occasion, establish that you would not like to work for this particular company. Finding that out before you have committed yourself to a job there is timely.)

And I don't mean a quick scan of their web site. It's always possible to get a better insight than that offered by a web site or a recruitment brochure, although either can be useful. The current recruitment brochure of accountancy partnership KPMG, for example, stresses their view of themselves as good corporate citizens:

> KPMG is not just focused on serving our clients. Our vision is to turn knowledge into value for

the benefit of our clients, our people and our communities. KPMG aims to inspire and facilitate our people to contribute positively to our society and create a sustainable business future. We recognise our responsibility for the social impact we have on communities and our corporate responsibility programme integral to what we do…

It's easy to get more information about a company by fishing around. You can ask questions of suppliers, former employees, environmental activists, local politicians and journalists. Almost everybody is happy to be asked for their help. Almost everybody likes to be seen as someone likely to be in the know. Almost everybody who finds that, in this specific instance, they're *not* in the know, will work particularly hard at working out who they might refer you to who would be in the know. Everybody in this country knows someone who will serve as a bridge to a company. You want to know the 'real deal' information about the company:

- What's it really like as a workplace?
- Constructive confrontation (Intel) or sweetness-and-light (Hewlett-Packard)?
- Is the boss the real boss, or is the place really run by someone else?
- Is it a family business failing to make the transition to a non-family business?
- Has the company recently experienced a dip in its share value or been thumped by the Environmental Protection Agency?
- Is it a business threatened by cheaper imports or positioned

to expand in the next few years?
- Does the company really value their employees or just talk about it and have pointless pub table quizzes once a year?

Another useful source of information – albeit only profit-and-loss data – is the Companies' Office. On their web site, some basic information is available free, and for a few Euro you can get any limited company's annual report, which will give you a clear picture of how indebted they are and how well they're doing.

Above all, what you want to know, before you encounter the recruitment officers of a company, is how it perceives itself. Most companies, when they set out to recruit, fill their advertisement with generalised claims to wonderfulness which don't actually give any real insight into their corporate reality. They claim to be innovative, responsible, respected leaders in their field. They announce that they are creative, committed to international peace and local prosperity and that they are equal opportunities employers. (They don't have a legal choice about being equal opportunities employers but it doesn't stop them presenting it as a virtue specific to them.)

As you continue in your preparation to ace the job interview, you should maintain your focus on their needs and ethos, not on your needs and preferences. Nothing should be said in your interview which does not position you as a solution to problems they have or challenges they face. They do not care that you want a job which allows you to go to university at night or travel for six months a year.

They will have laid out their requirements in the advertisement and in the job spec. Isolate each one of them and work out what, in your track record thus far, proves you have the capacity to deliver on each. If this is your first job, you will have little in the way of practical work experience but you may have undertaken tasks when at school or during work experience stints which demonstrate the characteristic sought.

Put the key words of each of the illustrations of competence on a separate slip of paper or small card and lay them face down on a table. Then write the key specifications on another set of cards and do likewise with them.

In the weeks before the interview, get into the habit of picking up one of the job spec cards at random and finding the card containing the perfect answer. Talk it out loud, although you don't have to, nor indeed should you, learn the answer off by heart. You just need to get your brain used to making the connection between the question and the content which proves you have the skill the question demands.

In time, you should be able to dispense with the cards of evidence, because every time you select a competence at random, the key data will automatically slot into place in your brain and emerge from your mouth.

Remember, throughout all this preparation, that you have to bring your CV to life. Do not hope or believe that the people interviewing you will have studied and internalised it.

'One of the most dearly held illusions,' Dr Arthur Freeman, who's written extensively about the mistakes clever people make in business, 'is that we know what others are thinking. "I don't have to tell him – he knows," is an all-too-common remark, and one that has a way of leading to disappointment when it turns out that he not only doesn't know, he doesn't even know you think he should know.'

It is your job, in the interview, to produce everything in your

CV and make it come alive to the interviewer, relating your experience and expertise to the job on offer. When job applicants don't do this successfully, the most frequent cause is an over-reliance on the capacity of the interviewer to extrapolate from an initial statement.

The interviewee says: 'I led a team of people in wheelchairs up Mount Everest.'

What she hopes the interview panel will deduce from that is that she's: a) a great fund raiser, because the money had to be found to transport everybody to the bottom of Mount Everest; b) that she's committed to diversity; c) that she is a lateral thinker, because making sure wheelchairs get traction on snow requires a bit of creativity; and d) that she's a good motivator, because, for most wheelchair users, just coping with Ryanair is enough of a challenge in any one year without Himalayas-climbing.

It does not work and it will not serve.

An essential truth of communication is that the onus is on the person transmitting data to make sure it's understood. Readers, viewers and listeners will never go the extra mile and work out what you're saying (if it isn't immediately clear to them) or its beneficial implications for them (if you haven't established those benefits). The other complication is a common misunderstanding of the value of experience.

Aldous Huxley once said: 'Experience is not what happens to you. It's what you do with what happens to you.' It is your job, as a job applicant, to make clear what aspects of any experience you have turned into expertise and how that expertise could now be useful to the company to which you are applying and the job you're seeking.

Break up any experience you want to quote into four segments:

1. What you did
2. How you did it
3. Insights or skills or competences you developed
4. How those insights, skills or competences are relevant to the job on offer

Think about it.

If you just do as many job applicants do, and describe number one above, they may decide you've lived through interesting times. So?

If you stop at number two above, they may decide you got your act together. That one time.

If you stop at number three, they may be impressed by you, but not quite clear on how this relates to the job they're trying to fill.

If, on the other hand, you go through the whole process, the discourse loops back to your understanding of, respect for, and applicability to their corporate demands.

Achieving all this, you will understand, takes a great deal of thoughtful and repetitive preparation. It does, however, change your position in the interview from hopeful, unguided missile into a focused, clear and productive presence. You should be able to come out after the interview, write down most of the questions asked and the gist of the answers given. You should do this after every interview. It reinforces learning. In the event that you don't get the job and – as you should – go back to the HR manager involved and ask for feedback on why they rejected you, you have built up a little file which can greatly help you when the next interview must be undertaken, there or somewhere else.

Notes made directly after an interview are also useful if you have to challenge the process subsequently. It's not likely, but every now and again, interviewees are asked inappropriate or frankly illegal questions in the course of a job interview and decide to take legal action to vindicate their rights. Their chances of winning their case are improved by having contemporaneous notes of the process.

A final key aspect of preparation is getting yourself geared up for the question you hope you won't be asked. The stinker question.

Good recruitment interviewers watch for discrepancies and gaps in a CV because those discrepancies and gaps can indicate time in prison, hospital or living under a bridge, none of which is likely to endear an applicant to the company. In addition, in recent times, good recruitment interviewers research candidates on Bebo, My Space and other web-based social networking sites. An applicant who figures on one of those web sites discussing precisely how drunk they decide to get each weekend is going to have a strike against them in the recruitment process. Every one of these social networking sites should carry a health warning: what you put up on this site about yourself will be read by people other than the people you currently want to impress and send a message about you, years down the line, you may not want sent to a prospective employer.

Whether it's a past firing or a gruesome self-reference on Bebo, be prepared for the possibility that the negative may surface in your job interview. Be so prepared that when it happens, it's welcome, rather than a stomach-creaser. Mentally acknowledging the possibility of being asked such a question does not amount to preparation for it. Contrariwise, it may simply hang a black cloud over your brain, distracting you from moving the rest of the interview on.

On the day, arrive in plenty of time. What to wear? Very

simple. Dress for the job you want, not the job you have. Wear the kind of clothes which the person in the role would wear. Bring a minimum of paraphernalia. Too many women reduce their impact at job interviews by carrying briefcases, handbags, folders and car keys. If you must carry all this stuff, leave the bulk of it with the receptionist. Don't bring your mobile phone into the room with you. And learn to walk across a room in a way that establishes confidence and authority.

Women instinctively, when crossing a room occupied by strangers, cross one arm over their body in a self-protective gesture. They do it unconsciously, often finding a subconscious reason to touch or fiddle with the strap of a shoulder bag. Don't do it. It diminishes your presence.

Teach yourself to walk across a room with your shoulders back. One hand can carry anything you need to bring with you. Imagine that you're carrying a heavy stone in the other hand. Curl your fingers around the imaginary stone and feel it pull your arm down straight. Then walk across the room, ready to shake hands. Whether you're right handed or a *ciotóg*, carry impedimenta in your left hand, freeing your right hand for a handshake.

Check out your handshake. Ask a friend to shake hands with you and if they tell you your handshake is akin to being offered a dead fish, fix it.

I prepare people for job interviews very rarely. The Head of our Careers Clinic, Eoghan McDermott, has a team of people who are kept constantly up to date about patterns of recruitment interviews. However, when the interview is a particularly high level one – for a CEO or hospital consultancy post – where an interview panel must be faced, I get to take part in a group interview of a VIP candidate. Every now and again, when I prepare a woman for a job interview, her biggest fear turns out to be the handshake, because she knows that, under pressure, her hands get wet and clammy. If you're one of those women, buy yourself unscented Mitchum antiperspirant. Ask your pharmacist to locate the version which comes in a jar in the form of a white cream. Rub it into your hands before the interview and you won't present a sweaty palm on the day.

The kind of questions you are asked at the interview will vary. What should never vary is the welcome you give them. Too many applicants sit anxiously awaiting each question as if they were students who had insufficiently prepared for an oral exam, thereby establishing themselves as unsure aspirants as opposed to obviously suitable future colleagues.

The interview panel is not your enemy. The panel and you have the same objective: to identify what skills and characteristics you have that qualify you for the job and will allow them to safely hire you. Your attitude, accordingly, should be that of a future colleague, rather than a mass murderer unwillingly providing the evidence qualifying you for the electric chair. Be open and welcoming.

But above all, listen. A member of an interview panel wants their question taken seriously. There's no premium on speed of answer. Indeed, by carefully considering an incoming question, you can indicate judgment. Let's say, for example, that a question is multi-clausal.

'Chairman,' you might say, 'the three elements of that question are equally important, but let me take the second first…'

Pausing to consider a question may also allow you to relate a question asked later in the interview with one asked earlier by another questioner, which illustrates your listening skills and your capacity to make links. It also pleases the person who asked the earlier question. But remember to answer all the sections of the multi-clausal question.

If you don't understand a question, ask for clarification. Never guess at what you think the questioner is after. You lose nothing by asking for a specific example to help you answer the question.

Similarly, if you don't have the answer to a question, do not fake it. Bunny Carr, the TV personality who started the company I first worked for, once advised that if you don't know the answer to a question, you have two choices.

'You can say you don't know the answer,' Bunny said. 'Or you can *prove* you don't know it. Much better to say straightforwardly that you don't know it.'

The Careers Clinic at the Communications Clinic provides a range of services related to job interviews. But they also put up on their web site useful information for free. In addition, the Head of the Careers Clinic, Eoghan McDermott, writes a weekly Career Doctor column for the *Sunday Tribune* recruitment page which is well worth consulting.

7

Appearance and Clothes

Dress [in the Middle Ages] sharpened social contrasts.
Some cities, by virtue of sumptuary legislation,
permitted just the gentle classes to wear silk or satin.
Fashion and colour, whether clothing appeared plain
or extravagant, bespoke age and occupation, as well
as rank.

A. Roger Ekirch, *At Day's Close* (Norton, 2005).

You may not remember Lucinda Ledgerwood. She's the girl who was fired from the 2008 TV reality show *The Apprentice* for being 'too zany'. One of Lucinda's hallmarks was that she liked to wear brightly coloured berets to work. She may be the first woman to have her career cut cruelly short by a beret.

It sounds and probably was a ludicrous reason for removing a contender. Many of the decisions made in reality TV shows are generated by the need for ratings rather than the realities which would obtain in any normal business. On the other hand, it has to be said that Lucinda self-evidently hadn't copped on to a key fact about clothes: they're a method of communicating that's as important as writing or speaking. Yes, of course, they serve more obvious purposes, like keeping us warm and preventing us from being arrested for indecent exposure. But once hypothermia and prison are obviated, the main – but largely ignored – function of clothes is to communicate. To communicate who we are. What we are. Where we come from. Where we're going. Where we belong.

Deriving therefrom is a problem for adolescents: finding a balance between dressing in an acceptable uniform (school uniforms are useful in this respect, in that they somewhat reduce wardrobe competition between teenagers) and rejecting what everybody else wears. Eager to learn whether this was an equal pressure on boys and girls, I asked a career guidance teacher for her view. She said it was a bigger pressure on girls. We moved on to other topics. But then, because she's also a bestselling novelist, the teacher, Mary Hosty, (www.maryhosty.com) thought some more and summed up one aspect of the issue as the pink feather pen syndrome:

> Some years ago, Reese Witherspoon starred in a delightful movie called *Legally Blonde*. It tells the story of a blonde prom queen ditched by her boyfriend. Abandoning her life of shopping, lap dogs and beauty treatments, she decides to follow him to Harvard Law School to win him back.
>
> I loved this movie but it's had a social influence far in excess of its cultural importance. Elle, the character in the movie, is delightful ditzy and cute. In a room full of serious-minded law students with serious looking legal notebooks and pens to match, she wields a pen with a large pink feather. This pen with the large pink feather has become a bit of a girly badge in recent years and to me it symbolises a lot of what can go wrong for young women as

they set out on a career path.

Unlike boys, young girls mostly were, mostly are and mostly will be made conscious of their image and the importance of it in negotiating the tasks of life. Society judges women,, in particular, on image and appearance and I don't think that's ever going to change. This poses particular challenges for young women – for instance how to project the best parts of their genuine selves whilst at the same time conveying an image of style and grooming, beauty perhaps, elegance and confidence certainly. It's a difficult and finely tuned balance and in the teenage years, girls often struggle to get it right.

If she opts to portray her genuine self at all costs she may risk overlooking the importance of appearance and image, resulting in the sort of people who retreat into a world of equally genuine people with similar non-hairdos, chipped fingernails, neglected waistline and slightly hairy legs, beautifully groomed dogs and elegant herbaceous borders. This is fine if she is self-supporting, runs a large fish farm or is lucky enough to be in a career where appearance doesn't matter at all. But it doesn't really work in large areas of life and career.

On the other hand, if she concentrates on image and appearance, suppressing her genuine self in favour of a carefully crafted, groomed and cultivated representation of what she would like to be and feels society expects, she risks losing herself in a mire of hair extensions, French manicures designer handbags, pink-feathered everything and shoe paradise, rendering herself incapable of real interaction with others, putting on a screensaver mask for the world and one day forgetting ever to take it off again. A real danger in over-focusing on image is that it can make us excessively self-conscious and distract our attention from more important matters. This is fine only if she's the latest Mrs Donald Trump and has Paul McCartney's eminently successful divorce lawyer.

But for most of us neither of these approaches to womanhood is to be recommended, most especially not in the career world. What we strive for is a balance; a smart professional appearance that indicates our attention to detail and our expectation that we will be taken seriously, together with a projection of the genuine parts of our selves that will help us to forge alliances and friendships, build strong networks, be approachable and dependable. It's probably best not to put that slightly racy sense of humour on display too often. Equally, strong, religious or political views are private matters and not relevant in most employment contexts.

And as for that pink-feathered pen – don't throw it away. Keep it at home. On quiet evenings, put on your pink fluffy slippers, curl up under your Lulu Guinness duvet in your Juicy Couture pjs and write up your diary. Written with care and diligence, it will be your truest expression of self and might make you millions when you retire.

(It's worth pointing out to readers that the advice about writing a diary does appear earlier in this book. And was written before Mary Hosty came through with exactly the same point.) Before we go back to the clothes issue, it's important to stress that a common delusion is that because something is interesting, we will remember it. Wrong. Wrong. Wrong.

A few years ago, a Professor of Law, Police Science and Criminal Justice at the City University of New York named Peter Moskos joined the Baltimore City police force for research purposes. In the evenings, he would make notes on what had happened during the day. Now and again, he would be too tired to do so.

'After a long night's work and a few beers, it was too easy to convince myself that memory would suffice,' he later wrote. 'Whatever I didn't write down is gone forever. Just one example: on May 28, 2001, I helped guard the crime scene of a twelve-person shooting.'

Six years later, when Moskos looked at his notes, the entry for the night was blank. The implication was painfully obvious.

'I thought I would never forget the details of a twelve-person shooting. Well, I have.'

Moral. Make notes. Keep a diary. Don't overestimate the functionality of your own memory. Its inadequacy is why God gave us Blackberries, computers and pens.

Taking Mary's point about pink-feather pens, we must admit that the nineteen-year-old who pitches up for work in leggings, a mini skirt, transparent top just short enough to reveal the tattoo on her lower back, Ribena-striped hair and an earring pinned through her nostril may not say much in the office, but her clothes speak for her. Loud and clear. Very loud and clear. Notice me, the voice of her clothes says. See how different I am.

Just how acceptable that statement is depends entirely on where she works. A business or organisation that's been around a long time and has developed a middle-aged hierarchy expects uniformity. In such an organisation, in the early days, little Miss Ribena will be viewed as an amusing diversion: isn't she a scream, all the same. (Although it has to be said that if she arrives for interview at a conservative company in her normal kit, the chances are she won't get the job in the first place.)

As time goes on, however, the organisation will make an inchoate judgement that this young woman is a recalcitrant outsider. Not only does she not follow the unspoken dress code – she can't be bothered to learn it. Or, worse still, is a social dyslexic who hasn't the wit to know there is such a code. If she's a social dyslexic, she's not promotable. Even at her present level, she may be an embarrassment at meetings. Her clothing announces her determination to serve her own needs before she gets around to meeting her employer's needs. So the employing body quietly sets about extruding her.

If, on the other hand, Miss Ribena goes for a job in a recent start-up company of independent-minded mavericks, providing a service like, say, event-management, she'll have no problem. Neither they nor their customers will be off-put by a nose-ring or a bright beret.

Women have much more latitude than men in what they can wear to work. Much more capacity for self-expression, courtesy of Topshop or BT. That's the upside. The downside is that nobody tells them what the boundaries are until they've crossed them.

The employer's assumption – and it's a fair assumption – is that career-building requires more than qualifications and diligence. It requires emotional intelligence. And if an employee doesn't have the emotional intelligence to read the language of the clothes worn all around them, they don't belong. The choice belongs to the employee. For Lucinda, that choice morphed into an ultimatum she never noticed: off with the beret or off with her head.

We may pay a lot of attention to the shoes Sarah Jessica Parker wears in the new *Sex and the City* movie, but we don't pay half enough attention to what our gear says about us to the people who matter to our future. The exception to this generality is terrorists. Terrorists concentrate fiercely on learning the language of clothes. After the attacks on the World Trade Centre towers, a search of the belongings left by Muhammed Atta and his comrades turned up a handbook giving them specific instructions in this regard. 'When you're in the outer world,' the booklet instructed, 'you have to act like them, dress like them, behave like them.'

It's obvious. As obvious as the fact that a company where all the bosses wear formal business suits is likely to look askance on an employee whose clothes are louder than they are and create a constant distraction. The employee, on the other hand, may dress in a way that speaks to their own preferences and have no interest in communicating a willingness to conform to the unspoken dress code. 'This is the way I am,' they may feel. 'I have an absolute right to be an individual in my self-presentation. Take me or leave me.'

The only problem with this admirable refusal to kowtow arises when the employee expects, despite the 'sod off' language of their clothing, to move up the ranks.

It sometimes works. Now and then, a woman who looks like an unmade bed or a leftover Goth will make it to the top as a CEO of a big company or as, say, a partner in an accountancy company. It's rare, though. The woman involved has to be so exceptionally able that how she looks becomes a factor to be ignored or tolerated, rather than a disqualifier. One such able woman was actor Sarah Bernhardt. Bernhardt continued to play romantic leads in her late forties, despite the fact that by that time she looked her age and was missing a leg. She was such an impelling presence on stage that she could convince an audience she was young, able-bodied and beautiful.

Making a statement through your clothes can be fun. Making too loud a statement can be counter-productive, in career terms. It's counter-productive to be referred to as 'That one with the Ribena hair and the nose ring' as opposed to 'Whatshername, the one who dragged that project in on time when we thought nobody could.'

The curious thing is that during the rest of the year, women in business dress like – well, women in business. Then May arrives, the sun comes out, the birds start to sing, the weather gets warm and many women in business develop amnesia about how to dress for success. Instead of the sharply-tailored black suits and the crisp white shirts worn during the winter, horrors like the muffin top and the tramp stamp emerge.

Muffin tops are where a woman's 'love handles' or 'flanks' (as the cosmetic surgeons call them) hang out over the top of their trousers. Tramp stamps are tattoos on the lower back, visible when a woman stoops to take something out of a filing cabinet or a desk pedestal.

According to one recruitment web site's research, 71 per cent of executives believe that wearing casual summer clothes to the workplace is a serious career error for women.

Nevertheless, it happens every year, as soon as bluebells replace daffodils in the garden. Women abandon the standards they apply at other times of the year and dress down. It may be the heat. Facing a day in the office in a jacket and trousers in mid-May can begin to look like duty, whereas the prospect of slipping into a frilly minimal sundress takes on a new appeal. It's cool. It's pretty. It lets the Bank Holiday tan show.

And it's a career disaster, no matter how many compliments flow from the lads in the office.

Compliments indicate appreciation of a sexy appearance. Promotion indicates appreciation of performance and competence. Rarely do the two march in tandem. The manager (male) who does a wide-eyed grin when faced with an expanse of glowing female chest is not often the man who appoints its owner to a senior position, in the longer term. Even in the short term, that man may decide to take a meeting with a client on his own, rather than bring with him the pleasing distraction of a summer-garbed female colleague whose presence might lessen the authority of the brand he presents.

Women lose their marbles, coming into the summer, in terms of career-friendly clothing, for a number of reasons, not least of which is the outbreak of 'holiday-itis'. This is a seasonal corporate disease kicked off by the May Bank Holiday. The symptoms start with the return of office-workers from that long weekend, when they stand around the water-cooler or in the cafeteria, talking about what they saw and spent wherever they went and beginning to yearn for the longer summer holiday period. Then the childless and child-free brigade head off on holiday because they don't have to wait for school to close. The mood in the office changes. It doesn't move to complete irresponsibility but it becomes less serious.

Executives who don't have a business lunch grab their sandwich and beaker of coffee and head to the nearest park or canal or riverbank in the middle of the day. If they anticipate, early in the morning, the possibility of such an al fresco lunch, they think twice about donning the formal tailored suit. Or even the tights. Particularly the tights. On a brightening summer morning with the promise of high temperatures later on, the thought of clingy tights becomes positively repellent.

Deciding not to wear tights is the first step in the abandonment of business dress. Going without tights (or 'hose' as the Americans confusingly dub them) has a rake of consequences. It can get you into trouble, if your company has a dress code precluding naked legs, and many firms have precisely that kind of dress code. It has a strange, unrecognised link to Victorian times. Back then, seamstresses made a tidy income out of making little pleated skirts for the bendy mahogany legs of chairs, tables and pianos. It was felt that the opulent polished bulges of such legs, unconcealed, would stimulate random lust in the Victorian male, and so an industry came into being: leg-concealment for furniture. Leg-concealment for women was, of course, so totally *de rigueur* that, as one Cole Porter song put it, 'a glimpse of stocking was looked on as something shocking'.

These days, it's a glimpse of leg without stocking that's considered shocking. Many bosses regard naked legs in the office as *louche*.

'Naked arms are bad enough,' one manager says, 'but naked legs are half-way to being undressed. What's that got to do with the office?'

Failure to insert oneself in tights, first thing in the morning, may not break an explicit company rule. But it can have damaging consequences, especially if the legs thus revealed are pasty, stubbly or patchy with badly-applied fake tan. Even more so if the feet revealed have a pedicure-deficit. Unvarnished, untrimmed toenails turn a potential asset into a liability. Add hammer toes, a bunion or two, visible corns or, worst of all, half-hidden plasters protecting blisters from being rubbed against by high-heeled sandals, and south of the knees can become a disaster area.

One male manager with whom I consulted, a couple of years back, on a dress code for his company was bothered by anything to do with toe-visibility. He came over all weak and nauseated when a woman in his office wore low-cut shoes revealing the cleavage at the top of her toes. If he could have mandated knee-high boots for all his women, he would have. Fortunately, he got distracted by one of his senior male executives, who took, throughout the summer months, to wearing blue boat shoes to the office. Blue boat shoes emerging from the legs of an Armani suit are the wardrobe equivalent of following caviar with jelly and cream: not unpleasing in themselves but contextually odd.

Anything linen is a mistake at any time. Linen carries an aura of classy cool, and five minutes after it's put on makes the wearer look as if they've been sleeping under a bridge for a week.

For women, in summer, fake tan is a lethal wardrobe contaminant. A dingy bra-strap is bad enough. A dingy, copper-stained bra strap is horrid. In summer, career women should invest in tailored pastel cottons with lining. A sudden shift to a skimpy top that shares your tramp stamp with the world won't help you get promoted.

THE TEN WORST SUMMER DRESS MISTAKES

1. Whale-tails (G-string/thong visible over trouser tops)
2. Sunglasses worn like an Alice band. (Leave it to Gillian Bowler, who patented the look.)
3. T-shirts with provocative messages across the chest

4. Sandals worn with unpedicured feet
5. Cropped trousers
6. False tan stains on ankles/elbows
7. Short-sleeved tops if the wearer has flabby 'batwings'
8. Knit cotton tops tight enough to outline every flesh-roll
9. Bracelets picked up in Ibiza
10. Going bra-less

8

Height and Weight

Every day the fat woman dies a series of small deaths.

Shelley Bovey

I haven't got a copy of the yearbook produced by my class in the Holy Faith Convent, Clontarf, but I think I remember a caption under my photograph suggesting, not that I had boundless potential or was everybody's best friend, but that anybody who wanted to know anything about dieting and calorie counts should ask me and I'd have the answer. Inevitably, the picture under which this advice appeared showed me to be – as always – a whole lot fatter than any of the slim gorgeous girls who knew nothing about dieting, either because they didn't need to or because they were sneakily eating very little.

The caption underlined several realities, the first of which was that, if you're taller than other girls in your teens, you have one strike against you. You know the teacher arranging the girls in the photograph, the contestants in the debate, or the singers in the choir, will automatically put you in the back row while, with his or her teachery voice crooning, calling for the 'little ones' to line up in the front. You know that in a drama class, you'll play Anne Sullivan, not Helen Keller, or the Nurse rather than Juliet.

You know you'll be expected to take care of the smaller kids in the class if anything goes wrong, even though they might, in brain terms, be able to buy and sell you.

And you know you'll be expected to do better than they do in the exams, because, Gawd love them, their delicate little brains can't cope with the stress and they do much worse in exams than they should. As you get older, another variant comes into play: the fragile seven-stone woman who, always in the company of men, admires your height and flutters, 'I've always wanted to be tall…' This provokes a fountain of reassurance from the men while making the tall woman present feel like the metal guy Harry Crosbie plans for outside the 02 (the Point Theatre, to you and me) who will not only be 150 feet tall, but into whose orifices people will be able to enter to check out how his pancreas is today and observe the process of him eating a Danish.

Tall is tough. But tall can be triumphantly surmounted. Witness the most exciting and attractive woman seen on the fringes of politics since a forceful American President visited Europe and amusedly introduced himself as 'the man who accompanied Jacqueline Kennedy to Paris'. The current President, not only of France but of the European Union, is in the same position: move to one side, there, Nicolas, and let's see the Wife. (Or, in the case of the visit he made to Dublin after Ireland voted 'No' to the Lisbon Treaty, 'Ah, Jasus, Nicolas, why'd you leave yer wan at home? Will you bring her the next time, will you?')

Carla Bruni is a phenomenon unseen since Princess Di. Here's a woman who has been adopted by women of all ages all over Europe as a deep inhalation of fresh air on the style front, starting with that grey caped suit, ostentatious in the subtlety of its cut, worn to meet the Queen. She wears flat ballerina pumps so as not to make Sarkozy look like a garden gnome when she stands beside him, and manages to look good in them. She observes him with demure respect. Best of all, she sells papers and helps keep his face current.

Sarkozy came out of a messy divorce and with Formula One speed hitched himself to a stunning woman who is beautiful, stylish, talented and fearless. Instead of a carbon footprint, Bruni has a sulphur footprint. Europe can't get enough of her. Of her past – multiple affairs with once-glamorous sex symbols. Of her effrontery – one of her songs claims she's had thirty lovers in her forty years. Of her separate identity – her discs are selling as never before.

But, above all, she's demonstrating that being tall, even with a much shorter man as your mate, can be an advantage. (Being small can be a disadvantage, in career terms, but much more for men than for women. Statistics grimly establish that, for men, to be short is a major drawback in terms of the promotions they get and the money they earn. It's never overt enough for them to take legal action – for the most part, it's a subconscious prejudice, half-consciously applied by others. Although you will hear people – particularly men – say about another man that he has 'short-man syndrome' or 'Napoleon complex'. While smaller women tend to be petted and patronised more than their taller sisters, the negative career implications are less clear.)

Then there's the weight issue. Which takes two forms. The first is weight manifesting itself in one particular place, most problematically for women, in the chest area. The second is generalised body fat.

Let's start with the boobs. (You boys in the back row need to be very careful. If the wind changed, you'd be stuck like that: adolescence forever.)

One of the most impressive women I've ever met had a strange habit when she had to be photographed. Tall and voluptuous, she would almost consciously square her shoulders and stand or walk to her full height, which was bloody difficult, because her boss was a tiny man who seriously hated being a tiny man and who was thrown into a day-long tantrum by having to get his photograph taken on the flat with anyone taller than he was. (Steps were OK. Steps allowed him to gain the height he needed and the top man is entitled to the top step.)

I was due to have a meeting with this woman on a Thursday. On Wednesday, her partner telephoned and told me the venue for the meeting had changed. OK, I said, where do I go? He named the hospital. Nothing serious, he reassured. She'll tell you herself when she sees you.

As she duly did. She'd had breast-reduction surgery. Never having had much in the way of a bosom, I was scandalised. How could she not like wearing formidable D cups?

Easy, was the response. How do I count the ways, was the response. She listed them:

- - Always having to buy a jacket at least one size bigger than the skirt
- Always being looked at by men first (and frequently thereafter) at bust level
- Always being looked at with venom by the women who noted the direction of the men's gaze
- Always suffering back pain
- Always having to do a conscious 'Stand up straight and hump the begrudgers' reminder to herself, based on the advice of her mother, from whom she had inherited the magnificently unwelcome frontal structure

- Never enjoying low-cut dresses because, she assured me, too much of a good thing is no fun
- Plus, she added bitterly, having a (male) photographer tell her he'd have to use a wide-angle lens to do her justice

At the time – fifteen years ago – it was a startling decision. These days, breast reduction and other plastic surgeries are easily available, not that costly and, for the most part, as safe as any other surgery. (If you want to know more about cosmetic surgery, read my book, *Mirror, Mirror – Confessions of a Plastic Surgery Addict*. And if you're determined to submit yourself to a surgeon, make damn sure the surgeon is expert, highly qualified and does a critical mass of the procedure you want done.)

If you don't want to go the surgical route, learn not to do the big boob crouch. It doesn't conceal the fact that you are well endowed. It just establishes you have no confidence about it. Stand up straight and get on with it.

The weight problem has been around for decades but has been getting steadily worse, as a pressure on women, mainly because of TV.

Two psychologists in Canada, a few years back, decided to examine the difference between real women and women who make it on TV. Gregory Fours and Kimberly Burggraf, based at Calgary University, looked at the weights of actors playing key roles in about thirty sitcoms like *Friends*, *Seinfeld* and *Frasier*. Unsurprisingly, they found them to be significantly below average weight and height, when compared with the general population.

The occasional hefty woman, like Roseanne Barr and – much earlier – Mary Tyler Moore's side-kick, Valerie Harper

(Rhoda) may have been good for a laugh, but the laughter died throughout the late 1980s. Both actors eventually – in one case permanently, in the other sporadically – lost weight, despite the inevitable consequence that, once thinner, they were much less funny. Overweight women faded, as factors in American prime-time TV programmes during the 1980s.

Fours and Burggraf, looking at this trend, pointed out that, since teenage girls watch an average of two TV situation comedies a day, it stands to reason that such programmes, with their unrepresentative presentation of thin women, will have sent a clear message to the young viewers: thin is good, fat is bad.

If television is responsible for creating the concept of an ideal woman who is much thinner than a normal woman (remember, Jennifer Aniston had to lose weight before she could get a job on TV in the first place) it is also responsible for global sharing of unsafe ways to get to that desired state. Having established, throughout the nineties, that fat is unacceptable, TV stations moved on to the next logical step: the production of 'reality' series in which fat people lost weight through 'boot camp' collective action with humiliation thrown in for good measure.

The Internet plays its part, too. The Web is full of sites showing women (and, to a markedly lesser extent, men) in before and after shots demonstrating how it looks to lose ten stone, and how greatly the formerly fat woman's self-esteem has grown since she shed the extra weight. Of course it has. When you're fat, other people assume you to be lazy and stupid. Being thin has nothing to do with intelligence but being overweight subjects an individual to everything from shouted questions as to who ate all the pies to the outrageously invasive advice of perfect strangers, usually preceded with the remark that 'you have such a pretty face'.

The 'I'm better than you are because I'm thin' mentality showed up when John Prescott, the former Deputy Leader of the British Labour Party, confessed, in his autobiography, to an eating disorder. For years, he revealed, any stressful political situation would cause him to stuff himself with food and then throw it up. He was not, he ruefully remarked, a particularly successful bulimic: he never managed to get thin.

His revelations were followed by an interesting set of responses. First was the 'me, too' reaction, with male celebs in middle age or older announcing that they, too, had spent years vomiting up gorged food and suffering the consequent guilt, shame and loss of self-esteem. One of those celebs was Uri Geller, whose mental capacity to bend spoons fell short of helping him control his intake at mealtime.

The second reaction took the form of arguably the most disgusting set of cartoons ever published in British media.

The third was an outbreak of retrospective worry, on the part of one of the Conservative newspapers, that Tony Blair should have had so sick a man making major decisions whenever he was absent from the country.

The final and most pervasive reaction was to praise Prescott's courage in revealing all. It's that last one that deserves most examination. On the one hand, Prescott's revelations undoubtedly and demonstrably empowered men who had, up to now, believed themselves to be exceptional and isolated, in suffering a disorder publicly associated with young women. Because he'd gone first, they felt they could now admit to their problem and seek treatment for it. On the other hand, the very publicity surrounding the confession will have introduced the concept of bingeing and purging to people who may now try it.

Of course enough coverage, in print, on radio and TV and

on the Internet has been devoted to bulimia for the revelation that Prescott is a bulimic to come as a surprise, but not as such a surprise as to create a new wave of bulimics. But it may be worthwhile to examine the general acceptance that no aspect of a life should be regarded as private and that sharing of this kind of information, even if it carries negative consequences, is the Right Thing To Do.

A related topic has been bubbling on the Internet for some time. It's called 'diabulimia' and is the preserve of diabetics.

Before insulin was available in injectable form, a new sufferer from diabetes 1 would become aware that something was wrong with them when they experienced a raging thirst, night, noon and morning, accompanied by rapid weight loss. Pre-insulin, the only treatment available was dietary, with patients trying to eat foods their system could digest, as opposed to sugary foods. Diabetics cannot transform sugar into food for muscles and brain. It floats in the bloodstream and is excreted in urine. But, because the brain and muscles need sustenance, they draw it from within. First, the fat stores in the body are depleted. Then the muscles start to waste. Pre-insulin, diabetics died fairly quickly after initial diagnosis, effectively starving to death.

Insulin changed all that, and each of us now knows families through which diabetes runs, striking at random, skipping a generation, then coming back. Forty years ago, diabetics had rituals which became the property of an entire family. Food (slices of Hovis bread, for example) had to be weighed on tiny kitchen scales. The new diabetic was trained to inject themselves, practising on an orange. The family learned to watch for the symptoms that required fast administration of a lump of sugar because the injected insulin had done its job too enthusiastically. Today, except for 'brittle' diabetics who have difficulty controlling their condition, the weighing and measuring has become less obvious, and many diabetics carry pre-measured doses of insulin in little gadgets like fountain pens which allow administration of the hormone, even in company, without anybody noticing.

However, young female diabetics often remember with nostalgic pleasure the weeks when the illness first manifested itself in their lives. The sudden, effortless, loss of one, two or even three stone. The concern of parents about the new fragility of their previously sturdy daughter. The admiration of peers who assumed a new killer diet was in progress. The thrill of buying jeans two sizes smaller than those worn beforehand.

A few of those diabetics, once treated, could not bear the weight gain that ensued as insulin went to work. They figured that skipping the odd dose would help them control their weight. It did. They worked it out that skipping more than the odd dose would help them *lose* weight. It did.

Now, here's the rub. If that information had not been shared, the cohort of diabulimics would have remained small. But it was shared. One widely reported case study tells of a thirteen-year-old at an American summer camp for diabetics, who overheard the medical counsellors giving a lecture to two other camp-residents, who'd been caught skipping their insulin. The counsellors left the two in no doubt that their quest for thinness through insulin abuse would kill them, blind them or cause them to have limbs amputated in the future. The girl who overheard the diatribe heard all the warnings. But she embarked, straight away, on insulin abuse herself.

Because the word spread – particularly through the Internet – specialists in diabetic care now face growing numbers of insulin-abusers or diabulimics who, after ten or more years of playing with their medications, are experiencing the consequences.

'At thirty my independent life fell apart,' one thirty-eight-year old diabulimic has written. 'I woke one morning with a black splodge of Marmite obscuring most of the vision from my left eye. Then the pain started – pain that would wake me screaming from sleep. I now can barely walk, can't drive, have renal failure, high blood pressure, high cholesterol and frequent admissions to hospital with pneumonia.'

Discussing this issue with a researcher from a television programme, I found myself sounding like a one-woman censor. The researcher held the view that information must be shared, regardless of the consequences. That it is not for one group or individual to restrict another group or individual's access to objective data, even if they choose to do themselves harm by the use of that data.

She is right, of course. Except that, worldwide, a consensus exists that sharing information on how to create weapons of mass destruction goes beyond the limits of free speech and free information-sharing.

The old axiom was that free speech did not include the right to yell 'Fire!' in a crowded theatre, because it would cause a lethal race for the exits.

The problem now is that much of the available information – including the reading of this book – can deliver knowledge to which people have rights, but which might kill them…

All I can do is hope it won't be the case. Hope that any woman reading this book knows who she is and what she's worth, in career and relationship terms, before she considers the weight issue. And when she considers the weight issue, I hope she'll do it selfishly. If obesity is threatening your health, do something about it. No. Wait. I know you've been told that before. If you've spent a couple of decades grievously overweight and have managed only yo-yo gains and losses, you are both more and less fortunate than you would have been twenty years ago. Less fortunate, because more judgements are made against you because you are fat. More fortunate in the number of support services available, together with the possibility of bariatric surgery. That's the intervention which reduces the size of your stomach, thereby limiting how much you can eat. It's complicated surgery. It's not perfect in its outcomes. Some of those who undergo it have troublesome side-effects thereafter. Some manage to regain lost weight. But for many patients, it is a solution with more than one good outcome. Preliminary studies suggest that this kind of surgery may reduce the incidence of other ailments including cancer.

Sometimes, buddying-up with a pal or pals can be a good idea for someone who desperately wants to lose weight but finds it difficult to do so on their own. The principle of mutual support is behind all the Twelve-Step programmes for coping with addiction which have sprung from Alcoholics Anonymous. This kind of approach suits some people and very definitely doesn't suit others.

The minute we lose weight, we become pain-in-the-arse converts and, worse still, evangelists, wanting everybody else to do it our way. What way you decide to lose weight is important, all joking apart. Just because a diet is presented to you by an 'expert' who claims that it works and who seems to have all the relevant qualifications does not mean that diet is necessarily right for you. Any diet which promises weight losses of more than a couple of pounds a week and which doesn't involve change of lifestyle (meaning you getting off your ass and doing some exercise) can do damage to your health and is unlikely to result in long-term weight-loss.

What we have to do, about height and weight, is get real. If you're tall, stand up straight. If you're short, wear heels, vertical stripes and walk tall. If you walk into a meeting where the chairs adjust up and down, adjust the chair to make the most of whatever height you are. Vincent Browne's TV news programme is very odd in this regard. On the Thursday edition, they clump together four guests, who may – indeed did, the last time I was on it – range in height from skyscraper to cottage. The floor manager then alters the heights of the chairs to even everyone out. Just one more illustration of the inaccuracy of that comment that the camera cannot lie. In this case, it makes little people look the same height as tall people, which must lead to strange encounters in the real world: 'My God, you're teeny! I thought you were a six-footer.'

If you're overweight and upset by it, do something about it. If you're overweight and not upset by it, stay as healthy as you can, otherwise, but be aware of the outsize, one-size-fits-all prejudices you will encounter as you climb the career ladder. Or, in some cases, as you step off the career ladder. Many women who take a career break to stay at home with their children find it inordinately challenging to get back into the workforce, because most mothers are heavier after they give birth than they were beforehand and mothers feeding children at home put on weight.

If you're happy that way read no further. If you're miserable, regard the extra weight as a suit of armour you needed for the child-rearing years. Now that you are back in the workforce you may need a different, shallower form of body protection. No more. No less. Weight's on the outside. It's what's on the inside that matters.

9

THE BABY BOMB

Take motherhood. Nobody thought of putting it onto
a moral pedestal until a few brash feminists pointed
out, about a century ago, that the pay is lousy and the
career path non-existent.

Barbara Ehrenreich

I was back at work the day after my son was born. Aha, I hear
you say. Driven career woman. Exception. Not part of the group
of women Eddie Hobbs talks about, who automatically earn less
money because of their motherhood. Easy for her to maintain
her economic value.

Wrong. I just didn't have my dates right. The baby's arrival
surprised the hell out of me. I was convinced he was due two
weeks later. (When they looked at him, they said not only
was he not premature, he was overcooked.) My diary had an
appointment for the following morning. Made no sense to
cancel. The man I went out of Mount Carmel to interview, a
wonderful broadcaster nicknamed Fab Vinnie, who died at a
shockingly early age, was taken aback when he saw me, squeezed
into my jeans.

'I thought you warned me you were very pregnant?' he
asked.

'Baby arrived yesterday,' I replied.

He could think of no good response to that, and I had no follow-up, since the only issue I had about the newborn was that he had a dented head, due to forceps, about which I was extremely anxious, figuring he'd be bullied for lopsidedness when he went to school. They had assured me the dent would come out without panel-beating but I had my doubts. One way or the other, I didn't figure Vincent Hanley would find the baby's dinge interesting. So we got on with the interview, I typed it up back at the hospital, and there I was, back in the routine. (The baby's head took on a proper shape overnight and he became the most beautiful infant in the history of childhood. Also the most charming. I had long conversations with him about life, the universe and his father, and he proved to be a good listener.)

It was dead easy for me to stay in the business game, from that point on. My husband had been raised by a working mother and therefore assumed he was as responsible for nappy changes, comfort-during-colic and preventing the house from becoming a health hazard as I was. More to the point, I worked with a bunch of people who cared about my contribution, not my constant presence. My mother and father were eager to take care of Anton.

So it worked. It worked so well, I was always taken aback when journalists asked me how I balanced work life and motherhood. What was the problem?

And then I had an argument with a county manager. I gave this county manager a dig about having only one woman on his top team. He got quietly furious. Because, he said, he always promoted women. Some of his brightest people in areas like engineering were female.

'So why aren't they at the top?' I asked.

'When one of my female staff has her first baby,' he said, through gritted teeth, 'she comes back to work and nothing changes. Her career path is as promising as ever. When she has her second baby, she begins to leave at five. When she has her third baby, her family demands overwhelm her.'

He knew it shouldn't be that way. He just knew it *was* that way. Because of childcare availability and cost. Because of the myth of the 'supportive' husband. (The 'supportive' husband cooks and cleans and plays with the kids but still manages to work late, attend conferences, play golf and take career-enhancing overseas trips. The most supportive husband also asks out loud where his socks are.) Because women found it easier to abandon their ambitions than demand change in the workplace.

That was twenty-five years ago. The problem is still there. Some women – an increasing number of women, as revealed by the census in mid-2008 – are postponing having children into their late thirties. That census revealed that the number of women having babies in those years now – for the first time ever – exceeds the number giving birth in their late twenties. The average age for a woman in Ireland to give birth, according to the Economic and Social Research Institute, is now thirty-one. More women in the third decade are having babies than nineteen-year-olds are.

A 2008 survey from the US Census Bureau finds the same trend in America – with the added twist that one in five women in America remain childless all their lives; twice the number a generation back. The proportion of childless women is steadily growing. It goes up – over there – by about one percentage point per year.

The interpretation of these figures which immediately offers itself is that the women giving birth want to concentrate on their careers, child-free, for some time in order to establish themselves and avoid the situation repeatedly observed by the county manager quoted earlier. That's how the author of the American study, Jane Dye, presents the new data.

Morag Prunty, the novelist who writes under her own name and as Kate Kerrigan, had her only child when she was thirty-seven, having put it off, she told journalist Eithne Shortall writing in the *Sunday Times*, because she was too wrapped up in her career – and too fussy about the prospective father.

'I thought I had all the time in the world, until I was in my thirties,' Prunty says. 'It was the whole *Sex and the City* thing. I wanted to be madly, madly in love.'

The only downside to postponement for Prunty was difficulty in conceiving a second child, which perhaps explains why, although she sees nothing negative 'about having a kid when you're older' she feels women should be encouraged to have babies while they're younger.

On the other hand, if you're a bit older, you're less likely to be seduced by the motherhood of the tabloids.

Waves of publicity surround celebs who have babies. That publicity creates a picture of pregnancy and birth awash in delight and ease. The baby arrives, the pictures are sold to *OK* magazine, and the mother loses her baby weight in three-and-a-half weeks, courtesy of her expensive personal trainer and her in-house chef. After that, we see her frolicking with her infant in fetching poses. Like lying on her back, wearing hot pants, on a pastel blanket in a public park. Now you know and I know that celebs do not casually find themselves in public parks and that the snapper was tipped off advance that pics of glowing parenthood would be possible at x time in y location, and that the mother wouldn't have been in y location if she hadn't lost the baby weight and flown in her Madison Avenue hairdresser to take care of her roots – but we still, idiotically, compare ourselves to these mothers, despite the utter discrepancy in circumstances.

- We feel fat and inadequate.
- We feel fat and guilty.
- We feel fat and pressured, if we have another, slightly older child who starts wetting the bed in response to the arrival of what we have advertised in advance as a great new playmate.
- We feel fat and unsexy.
- We feel fat and sexually unwanted, even though a suggestion of a bit of the other is about as welcome as bubonic plague.
- We feel fat and got at by our mothers, who all know better ways to do the motherhood thing.
- We feel fat and fraught, because we planned to breast-feed and it doesn't work. (Or we feel fat and excluded because trying to breast-feed quietly is like blowing a police whistle in a library, it attracts so much disapproving attention.)
- We feel fat and dirty, because the baby keeps puking on us.
- We feel fat and furious because when we tell people the name of our offspring, they clearly don't think much of it.
- We feel fat and frumpy, because we don't want to continue to wear pregnancy clothes but we punish ourselves by buying cheapo transition clothes.
- We feel fat and desperate for sleep.
- We feel fat and resentful that the man in our life picks up the baby when it's screaming its little bald head off,

and the child immediately goes quiet, emitting the occasional sob to underline how badly we – its mother – have been handling it.

- We feel fat and ashamed because we don't always and immediately love the baby the way we thought we would.
- We feel fat and isolated.
- We feel fat and nostalgic for the days when we had a stomach as flat (as Walter Macken put it) as a table, and when we walked down the street imagining having sex with every man we met. (Now, we just annoy ourselves by remembering those days.)
- We may even feel fat and depressed, although we don't want to admit that.

Let's start with the depression. It happens. You don't cause it. It happens. Your body has just undergone a hormonal earthquake, you are exhausted, you're out of your normal context, learning new skills under pressure and coming to terms with another human being, a demanding new personality who can't be put on the naughty step or told to go play in the traffic and who has no sense that you are anything other than its servant, twenty-four hours a day. Depression is one of the body's responses to all that. Depression is not feeling a little overwhelmed or down. It's about feeling life is not worth living, that waking up in the morning is a trial beyond bearing, that nothing is worth doing, nothing is worth hoping for, that nobody else has ever experienced this slough of despond and that there is and will be no end to it. Ever.

One of the seminal books about this problem, Katherine Dalton's 1989 publication *Depression After Childbirth*, observes that depression and psychosis were less severe in the early part of the twentieth century. Now, admittedly, *all* depression was less severe back then, but the key difference for new mothers is that, back then, mothers were not sent home within forty-eight hours of birth, as is currently the standard. In those bad old days, mothers tended to stay in maternity hospital for up to a fortnight. Tut tut, we'd say today. But the reality was that those new mothers were surrounded during that time by supportive staff who gave them help to come to terms with the new experienced and its demands. They had time to get to know their new family member and, above all, they got rest, sleep, nutritious food and encouragement. Small wonder they suffered less from depression.

The civilised world now knows that seeking the right medical intervention for post-partum depression enables a woman to fulfil her potential as a mother, while fighting it without help endangers her and her baby.

No matter how happy and healthy the mother or her child, the reality is that nothing is ever the same again once a baby has entered a household. Some women who planned to return to the workplace immediately after giving birth get overwhelmed by the experience and cannot bear to leave their baby. They extend their maternity leave. They take unpaid leave. They take a career break. And, eventually, they make the decision not to go back to work until their child is at school. Or later.

Some of the new mothers who opt to stay at home do it out of a conviction that there's no point in having children and then outsourcing their care to third parties. They want to be there when their toddler speaks her first word. (I was not there when my son spoke his first word. His grandmother was the witness. 'Car!' he said enthusiastically, pointing out the window at the traffic.)

On the other hand, mothers who soldier through the first couple of years, packaging their baby and its belongings up in the dark dawn hours before driving the infant to a crèche prior to going to work, may lose heart when the toddler gets a little older and starts to complain about the early start or the late pick-up.

Whether out of informed conviction or exhaustion in the face of the whole childcare choreography, some women decide to go home. Fewer and fewer women, however, are taking that option. In Britain, for example, the number of stay-at-home mothers has dropped by a quarter over the last fifteen years. The reason? For the most part – and this is borne out by anecdotal Irish experience, too – it's financial. In the heady days after Women's Liberation, when, in the 1970s, the European Union put laws on the statute book defending a woman's right to keep her job when she married – as opposed to the old civil service deal where you were out the door as soon as you had plighted your troth – and banning workplace discrimination against women, working outside the home was seen as a self-fulfilling choice. Now, for many couples, it has become a necessity.

'One of us would have to be earning in excess of fifty thousand euro a year for the other to stay at home with the kids,' one mother in her early thirties told me. 'And, I mean, *well* in excess of fifty thousand. Probably more since inflation started again – our mortgage is going up all the time. We keep talking about me taking a few years at home with the children, but when we do the sums, it really doesn't seem possible, and I don't mean we'd be worried about a drop in living standards. We're not Ferrari-and-villa-in-Florence people.'

If she does get to work at home – oops, sorry, work in the home – she'll quickly have to come to terms with the downsides of her brave decision. That very phrase, 'work in the home' touches on part of the downside. The moment a mother or father leaves the workforce to work at home, they encounter the personally-offensive question 'Oh, you don't work, then?'

They would say they work harder than most people in offices do. One of the most formidable women I know, who was a top manager in a major state-sponsored body before she decided to take time at home with her three small children, is up at dawn and is usually the last person in the household to hit the sack. She is in charge of feeding and transport. Those two tasks alone take up hours of every day, as she delivers one child to primary school, two to different secondary schools, then later picks them up and delivers them to ballet, music and sports venues.

But she is also in charge of household repairs, whether that's a slate off the roof, an airlock in the radiator or a faulty door on the washing machine. She's responsible for washing, dry cleaning and ironing. She pays bills, balances the budget, takes the pets to the vet when they're off colour and once every day visits her mother, who is in the advanced stages of Alzheimer's. By any measure, this woman is a hero. But that's not how she experiences other people's view of her.

'When we're at a party or a dinner in a friend's house, the woman or man next to me, sooner or later, will ask me what I do,' she says. 'When I say I work in the home, their eyes glaze over. They don't even bother to conceal the degree to which they've made the decision that I must be boring, never doing anything interesting, and might possibly bore them with some cute kiddie story.'

Because she has the radio going all the time, she's probably better informed about current affairs and politics than any other guest at a dinner party but she rarely gets asked her opinion.

If a financial value were allocated to all the tasks this woman completes in her ninety-hour working week, www.salary.com, the Massachusetts firm that computes typical salaries, says she should be paid around eighty thousand a year. She wishes…

Although one government, a couple of decades back, made a foray into paying women who stayed at home taking care of their mate and their offspring, it never came to anything much, not least because the boom years of the Irish economy made it imperative to get women out of the home and back into the workplace. Women who went back into the workforce rarely abandoned all their home responsibilities, because few of them were paid enough to afford full-time home help, and their menfolk were helpful – but only up to a point, as journalist Áilin Quinlan observes.

> Women, no matter where they live in the world or what they do for a living, inevitably end up doing the lion's share of the housework. In Ireland, men do an average of about nine hours of housework a week compared to more than twenty-one hours notched up by women. Researchers also found that married men here do significantly less housework than men who live with their girlfriends but aren't married. In America, researchers have found that having a husband actually creates seven more hours of housework a week for a woman.

Just why a husband would do less work in the home than a live-in partner isn't clear. What is clear, however, is that working in the home is simply not valued, according to Joanna McMinn, Director of the National Women's Council.

'If it was valued,' she points out, 'you would have policies in place that would support parental leave and paternity leave; that would make it easier for families to make choices.'

The families – although they lessen with every passing year – who decide that the mother should opt out of office work for a few years regard the decision as problematic but positive. For the company employing her, it's a different story. I was in an office recently where a male executive said that if he ran a small company, he would never employ a woman 'of childbearing age'. The near-lynching which ensued was a joy to watch. He'd made his comment to four women, only one of whom had a baby, but all of whom were very much of childbearing age.

It was outrageous, they said. It was probably illegal to say what he'd said, they told him. It would certainly be illegal to act on his viewpoint. Plus, one of them finished, he was a male chauvinist pig of a kind that should have been stamped out years ago.

The young man involved, unfazed, shrugged and said that if he'd divvied up the money to set up a small company, he would be a rotten businessman if he didn't focus on shareholder value. Employing women who were likely to leave the workplace to have babies was a real and present endangerment to shareholder value. Furthermore, he added, when he employed people (if he was employing people) he would want them committed to his company.

'At the expense of their right to have a baby?'

'Yes,' he said. 'You can't have it all. Nobody can. I can't frig off to Australia for eighteen months if I want to make partner. I can't concentrate on becoming a scratch golfer. I'd like to go to Australia and I have the potential to be a scratch golfer but I made adult choices, based on the priorities I have set out for my life. If you want to have babies, by all means have babies.'

'Thank you for your permission.'

' – but don't fool yourself that you can have babies and take three months out of a working year and that it will have no consequences for your employer or for your own career path.'

'So any ambitious woman has to stay childless?'

He shrugged.

'The solution is to change workplaces to value and use a woman's skills, ability, insight and contribution as they should be used and allow her to fulfil her rights as a human being,' one of the women told him, gathering her briefcase and leaving, I suspect because if she didn't, she'd have belted him upside the head with the same briefcase.

It's easy to dismiss what he said as typical of the male chauvinist he was immediately categorised as. But this kind of thinking isn't confined to male chauvinists.

Rosie Boycott, the feminist who, thirty seven years ago, co-founded *Spare Rib*, an aggressive advocacy magazine for and about women, unexpectedly found herself in the same frame of mind in recent years. Boycott moved from journalism to running a small farm, whose finances she describes as 'fragile' enough to have her worried, as the end of each month comes up, about how to pay the bills, including the salary bills for the farm's few employees. She wrote in the *Sunday Times*:

> As a feminist, I've believed that women should have the right to work, if that is what they want. I've also always believed that employers should stand by their female staff when they have children, that maternity leave and maternity pay should be just as much of a given as our right to a pension. But when

the British MEP Godfrey Bloom blustered that 'no self-respecting small businessman...would ever employ a lady of child-bearing age,' I found myself in a dilemma.

The dilemma for Boycott is that if one of her young female employees gets pregnant, she (Boycott) would have to pay her for a full year after she'd given birth, and Boycott couldn't afford that. But that's not the end of her internal conflict. She herself worked mostly at home in the eighteen months after her daughter's birth and recognises that many women today wish to work part-time once they have children. The problem is that the pigs on her farm require feeding at specific times each and every day, so two- and three-day weeks for her employees make no sense:

> How on earth, after thirty-five years of fighting for our rights to work and to be mothers, did we reach such a sorry state of affairs? Having children is, after all, the country's most essential job, yet from every direction, women are being slapped and punched by red tape and angry employers...the social breakdown we are witnessing starts from the moment our children are born into a world which is hostile to mothers. But I'm also painfully aware it is equally hostile to the managers of small businesses. Why should they be the ones who have to pick up the pieces when mothers take long maternity leaves or insist on flexible working practices that leave everyone else with more to do? It makes the childless resentful, and it makes employers angry...

Some larger organisations – the ESB was one of the earliest – have made an enormous effort to make the workplace family-friendly, although in real terms, this tends to mean 'mother-friendly' since so few men, still, take on parenting as a central role.

Changing the workplace in order to free up the potential of women has happened in some large companies and organisations that have a commitment to equality and the money to deliver on it. But when it comes to getting crèches and flexible working hours into all places of employment, particularly into smaller companies, don't hold your breath.

It's not that those companies are not sympathetic to the complex aspirations of women, or that they want to shove the responsibility on to the individual woman. It's just that, for smaller, newer companies, as Rosie Boycott honestly delineates, it's a practical problem. They may not have the numbers of mothers with small children to justify the setting up of a crèche, or they may be put off by the costs, insurance implications and space requirements.

Discussing this issue in the office vacated by the assertive male who wanted no part of employing women of childbearing years, I was fascinated by the bewilderment the youngest mother present demonstrated. 'Nobody tells you the truth about having babies,' she complained.

'Childbirth, you mean?'

'Well, that, too. Nobody tells you that a baby just turns your life inside out. It's like you emigrated from real life and they won't let you back in. Ever.'

One of the single girls shrugged and said there were lots of childcare facilities now available, only to find herself crisply told off by one of the older women, who was able to list the costs of just one heavily branded childcare chain, which would have wiped out most of the young woman's salary. This set her back a bit. Then she rallied.

'Yeah, but even if someone had told you all that,' she said to the mother of the toddler, 'you'd have still had Jessica. Wouldn't you?'

Jessica's mother nodded miserably, conscious that it had been her half-joking, whole-in-earnest murmur that she and her husband were thinking of having another infant that had sparked the original comments about not employing women of childbearing age.

It doesn't help that, as day follows night, every year brings at least one rash of newspaper stories that take every employer off the hook, by portraying women as not interested in careers at all. Women, according to these reports, want to be at home minding their kids and filling the house with the scent of freshly-baked bread.

Sometimes, the catalyst for this 'going native in motherhood' flurry of coverage is the early retirement of some reasonably well-known businesswoman who gives it all up in order to stay home with her sprogs. Media go nuts over her, transforming her, before you could put a nappy on a newborn, into a trend. She's not on her own, they sagely opine. Most women really, really would do the same, if they had the chance. Nature will out. The hand that rocks the cradle rules the world.

At other times, the story flows from a survey, like the one published by *Red* magazine in 2008, where a majority of young women claimed that, given a choice, they wouldn't go back to work once they started having babies. Most of the respondents to the *Red* magazine questionnaire really wanted to be domestic goddesses, they claimed. Like Nigella Lawson.

All over Britain and Ireland, radio stations fell on the survey with glad cries, because it allowed them to put women on the air giving out about the awful driven females who have lost touch with their real nature and think that driving a Ferrari is what matters.

Despite the level of coverage this kind of survey gets, the truth is that most women don't have a choice. Even if they have children, or, frequently, *because* they have children, they have to work. It's not about a Ferrari and having to work doesn't mean that they're driven or have mislaid any aspect of their femaleness.

Any survey of this kind is self-selecting: you get responses from the age, gender and attitude you'd expect from the women who read the magazine. I'm not saying *Red* is an update of *Woman's Own*, but you won't find that many young accountants, lawyers and entrepreneurs reading it. Instead, you get the young women whose jobs are mind-bendingly boring and who rightly dread trotting into the plant every day to sit in their cubicle like Dilbert in heels, dreaming about the weekend or their next holiday.

They know that the minute they start having babies, their lives will be a nightmare cross between logistics manager and chauffeur, packing cute baby bags with nappies and nappy-rash cream and sterilised bottles before heading off in the cold and the dark at dawn to drop the infant at a crèche and doing the reverse in the evening, sweating bricks at the possibility of being delayed by traffic and having to pay a fine to the child-minder.

Do those young women dream the dream of domestic goddess-hood? You bet they do. And rightly so. Except for one thing. Well, maybe more than one thing.

For starters, unless she picks a seriously rich bloke, the girl who dreams of being Nigella needs to produce a salary to cover mortgage, car repayments and all the other increasingly costly expenditures of joint living.

But even if the rich bloke is available, the wannabe Nigella shouldn't forget what her mother and grandmother knew: once you don't generate and control your own money, a partnership can shift. You can't buy a beautiful bag without a) lying to the provider about its cost or b) feeling grateful and guilty. Grateful and guilty are not happy emotions.

In addition, all the more serious studies, done over a long period of time with truly representative samples of women, should switch on a lot of red lights. Because those surveys show that women who spend a long time at home minding their kids sooner or later want to get back into the workforce, if only because they're sick of other women going glazed when they ask 'What do you do?' and get told about roasting potatoes in goose fat.

Except – and here's the problem – when they decide to go back to the office, they've become less skilled in what makes an office tick. They're not up to speed on software or management practices. Worst of all, they've lost confidence. They feel fatter, slobbier and less worthwhile than the women who crèched out of the total child-minding experience.

Fair? Of course not. But sometimes the truth isn't fair.

And, while we're on the subject of unfair truths, can we address the Nigella dream? Nigella may be on her own in front of the camera, but she sure as hell isn't on her own, otherwise.

Having a good support army makes being a domestic goddess pretty damn easy. Being Nigella on one (ordinary) salary without a support army is pretty damn hard.

None of which removes the visceral female conviction that

having a baby or a second baby or a third baby is essential to her happiness, or the related belief that if she stayed at home for several years, cooking meals from scratch, reading to her offspring and – a little later – ferrying them to art, music and rugby camps and classes, they would be the happier and most accomplished kids of their generation and she would feel content and fulfilled.

That dream can become a reality. For some women. And there's no point in warning off the other women for whom it definitely will not become a reality. Because the inchoate urge to have a baby or another baby is way beyond disputing. It's a neural cue central to the survival of the species and there's no arguing with it.

We can point out to you that if you're in that frame of mind your life will be changed by having a baby. It's not like buying a goldfish tank with inhabitants swimming around. It's more like having a bomb tossed into the middle of everything you do and say and are. There's no managing it. It rearranges everything. Sometimes for the better. Sometimes not.

A recent survey by www.workingmums.uk, for example, found that:

- 53 per cent of mothers say they lack confidence after an extended period out of the job market.
- 90 per cent felt that it is very difficult to find flexible work, although the vast majority wanted this so they could balance work and family life. 83 per cent feel that it is hard to find flexible jobs which use their skills. 95 per cent said childcare was very expensive and 88 per cent said there were not enough

flexible childcare options available. 39 per cent of mothers who didn't work said high childcare costs were a factor.

- 74 per cent said they felt guilty about leaving their children while they worked and 61 per cent worried that their children suffered because they worked.
- 55 per cent of survey respondents said employers have little or no understanding of the challenges facing working parents.

None of that – and it's pretty close to the reality experienced by working mums in Ireland – is the fault of the baby. What it points to, however, is that if you have a baby in this imperfect world with its imperfect workplaces, partners and childcare arrangements, you are, from that point on, are at the behest of someone else in a way that's unimaginable when you're single and child-free. And you can't put a baby back where it came from.

10

Moving up through the Ranks: Reviews and Promotions

Some people were critical of me, saying that I was overly-ambitious. Being 'ambitious', of course, is something they do not say about a man with the same qualities. Adjectives that are applied to describe certain characteristics are positive when referring to a man, but are viewed as negative when applied to a woman.

Madeleine Albright, Former US Secretary of State

When Cherie Booth, now better known as Mrs Tony Blair, got her degree and started to work in a legal firm at age twenty-two, she quickly spotted that her gender was likely to do her career progress no end of harm.

That year only 16 per cent of those of us called to the Bar were women. The year before it had been 9 per cent and the year before, even fewer. Yes, the percentage was growing, but attitudes among senior barristers – the people who would decide who got tenancy – were not. A set book in my first year reading law was *Learning the Law* by Professor Glanville Williams, QC. In the 1973 edition he warned of the difficulties of women succeeding at the Bar. 'Practice at the Bar is a demanding task for a man,' he wrote. 'It's even more difficult for a woman. It's not easy for a young man to get up and face the court; many women find it harder still. A woman's voice does not carry as well as a man's.' His advice to women was 'become a solicitor'. I will never forget how, shortly after I was called, an entire robing room full of men fell silent in shock and horror when it dawned on them that I was going to go in there and change into my wig and gown along with the chaps...

Cherie Blair, because she was a stroppy ambitious working-class girl who never knew her place and never intended to try to learn her place, overcame that prejudice, just as later she coped with the problem, as a Queen's Counsel (roughly the equivalent of an SC in Ireland) of taking cases which required her to argue in court against her husband's government, with the inevitable media fallout.

Her lifetime spans a period of massive change, in Britain and Ireland alike. If, today, you flip through the pages of the IPA *Diary* (which every ambitious woman should have on her desk) you'll find women who are directors general of government departments, CEOs of local authorities, directors of this or that quango. Move away from public administration, and you'll find big accountancy firms like KPMG and PWC have female partners, as do all the major law firms.

But if you opened the edition of the IPA *Diary* published the year Cherie Blair started to practise law, you wouldn't find one woman as secretary to a government department or as manager of a county council. Nor did accountancy firms have female partners.

In the interim, we've made enormous yet somewhat limited progress. Look again at the sections on government top bods, and you'll find the women stand out because of scarcity. Same deal when it comes to county managers. Even at the top of the state-sponsored bodies, men still predominate.

However, if you move slightly down the ranks in any of these organisations, you will find the reverse. The head of HR, of communication and perhaps of other functions will be female. Many of those successful women (although not all of them) have husbands or partners and have children, yet have managed to make progress in their careers. Many of them are pleasant, happy, likeable people.

I mention this last because the abiding stereotype of the woman who makes it through the ranks is one of a driven bitch. I call this the Gillian Bowler syndrome.

I first encountered the Gillian Bowler syndrome when I was appointed to a state board. They sent me a list of the people already on the board. Prominent lawyers. Industrialists. Trade Unionists. All male. Just one female. Gillian Bowler, the woman who – sunglasses holding back her long, dark hair – turned her company, Budget Travel, into a resounding success and sold it off for millions.

'Oh, hell,' I thought. 'That Gillian Bowler's going to be a hard bitch. I'm going to hate this.'

I didn't and she wasn't.

The woman who went on to serve as Chairman of Fáilte Ireland for some of its best years until she chose to step down in 2008, and who currently chairs Irish Life & Permanent, turned out to be a funny, warm and generous person. Good listener. Plus, she scattered a bag of Milky Mints on the table at the beginning of each board meeting.

The belief that to get to the top in business, politics or the public service, you have to be a hard, driven, inhuman bitch is so pervasive, it serves to deter young women from being as ambitious as they should be. Who wants to get to a position where other women assume you have to be a Godawful diva? Or where – as happened to me this year – you find yourself described in print as 'fiery and difficult'. *Moi*? Easygoing slobby *moi*?

As Madeleine Albright points out in the remark quoted at the beginning of this chapter, the world views ambition in a woman in a quite different way from how it views ambition in a man. Men are supposed to be ambitious. Women are not.

Except that some women are ambitious from an early stage. Take my friend Cindi, in Florida. I encountered Cindi when I wanted to save myself time in the morning by having eyeliner and lipstick already applied, courtesy of permanent make-up. Permanent make-up, where they tattoo your lips red and a navy line on your eyelids, is now available in Ireland, but ten years ago, when I had it done, Cindi was recommended to me by a cancer surgeon in the US.

'Her mother had cancer and lost her eyebrows through chemo,' he told me. 'Cindi decided she was going to learn how to do permanent make-up for cancer patients. She does it for other people too.'

When I met Cindi, I discovered that one of her markets is made up of people who get a tattoo, thinking they'll look like Angelina Jolie, and a few years later decide they look frankly tacky and want the thing removed.

She has one regular client who, when he goes on the tear, gets himself tattooed and when he sobers up, comes to her to have his indiscretion removed. He goes on the tear quite a lot. But when he needs tattoo-erasure, he has to wait a few days, because Cindi does permanent make-up on only one day a week. The rest of the week, she's a property developer.

When she was a kid, sitting in the back of her father's car, listening to her parents talking, Cindi would look out at the passing scenery, craning to see the tops of office blocks and thinking 'When I grow up, I'm going to own buildings like those.'

Not your average toddler's ambition. Not the ambition of the beautician she later became. But in America you can be anything you want and as soon as she had enough money saved, and enough of a track record with a bank to justify them trusting her, she bought a building. Not much of a building. A residential building, into which she put renters.

The way she says 'renters' says it all. There's people who own their homes. There's people who rent their homes. She may value them as customers but she has no time for what she calls 'renter mentality'.

In 1995, she bought her first office block. Her husband's company specialised in refurbishments and remodelling, so whenever she bought a property, he and his guys moved in to make it beautiful.

As well as buying property, she bought land.

'Not makin' any more of it,' she would shrug, having bought a plot of land out in the boonies. It would take years, she knew, for suburbia to subsume that area but the purchased land could sit, untended, for the duration. Sooner or later, because this was Florida, people would come. Three-quarters of the ageing population up north wanted to spend their latter years in a warm place, and as they moved south, the young service industry people would move in too. Even if she did nothing with the land, it would grow in value with every passing year. Just sitting there, it would make her richer.

2005 saw the first slowdown in that growth. 2006 ground it to a complete stop. Nobody was buying. Nobody was moving. Ergo, nobody was developing or selling. When the first quarter of 2007 saw no improvement, she put a name on the situation. Recession.

'Soon as economists begin to talk about "averting" or "minimising" a recession, you're already three to six months into an actual recession,' is how she puts it. 'When it started, I figured it would last to end 2009. Lately though, I figure 2011, minimum. I sat down and thought it through. In a recession, folks stop buying big stuff. But they don't stop buying little stuff. In fact, they're *more* likely to buy little stuff to compensate for not being able to buy big stuff. So I bought a pewter factory.'

The pewter factory makes ornaments, mazes and charms for bracelets. Pewter is light and cheap compared to more precious metals but does not rust or tarnish, so it's grand for letter-openers (why anybody would want one boggles my mind) sports trophies, corporate desk gifts and Christmas tree ornaments. She learned everything that could be learned about pewter, started to attend gift and ornament shows and parlayed her wares into several international gift catalogues. Between now and 2011, she and her husband will remodel the properties they've bought, holding them against the day when the recovery begins. In the meantime, the little pewter items will keep the cash flow going.

The advantage Cindi has, of course, is that she started her own business. She is not dependent for the money she makes, the title she holds or the level she reaches on the approval of other people. She can be ambitious without rubbing anybody else the wrong way. But the point is that many women in medium or large businesses they do not own, even if they take detours into social life and involve themselves in marriages and childbearing, nonetheless want to make progress. They are ambitious.

However, in many large organisations, factors come into play which slow the progress of women. One of them is what's been called the 'pink collar ghetto'. That's the area within large businesses where women tend to cluster, and out of which it can be difficult to be promoted. Areas like HR, PR and marketing sometimes hold disproportionate numbers of women. That's not a problem, except in organisations where people with an economics, finance or engineering background tend to be promoted to the top. If you're in this kind of business you have to work extra hard – perhaps doing a degree at night in one of the favoured disciplines – in order to break out of what at first looked like a promising division.

Some organisations quite simply favour men at the top. They're not supposed to. They don't do it overtly. They stay within the law. But they do it. If you're in such an organisation, you have to be realistic and decide if you have the stamina for a long, sustained battle. It may be easier to take your experience and your ambition and apply them elsewhere.

That said, however, the fact is that many women who fail to make progress sustain themselves with the male bonding myth: the belief that all men play golf in order to get the suss on each other's business and stay in a golden circle that excludes women. Nonsense.

What men do – and what women need to do more of – is socialise upwards. Women socialise downwards. Promote a woman in business and her major problem tends to be how to stay friends with the pals she's left behind at a lower level and prove to them that she hasn't been changed by moving up the career ladder.

That's a pivotal and too often ignored factor in women not making it to the top: the fact that when they get promoted, they are unable to move into a more managerial style. Yes, the fashion for the last couple of decades has been to eschew the word 'manager' in favour of the word 'leader' and to imply that nobody gives orders any more, but – particularly in tough times – organisations that must increase their profits or their efficiency need managers who can move the entire organisation along, rather than stay bosom buddies with their former peers.

The other factor that tends to make women less promotable is the travel issue. I am frequently consulted by companies which have short-term overseas placement needs. They might, for example, require an engineer to move to China for six months to oversee the transfer to a plant there of a manufacturing line it's now too expensive to make in Ireland or anywhere else in Europe. Those companies are baffled by the gender problems they run into when they offer the post (which carries all sorts of perks and future progress built into it) to the most relevant woman. One manager told me recently:

> The response of women to the requirement to travel is a constant disruption of our business planning. I have no idea how to address it without it becoming an unpleasant equality issue, but the fact is that right now, it's a hidden equality issue. Male executives who have children, for example, are much more likely to end up on overseas assignments than women with

children, and even within Ireland, where we have
three plants, women are less willing than their male
counterparts to do even the minimal travel required
to undertake quality control work in the other
plants. Now, fine, some of the men have a preference
for doing this kind of trip but not all of them do.
However, when push comes to shove, the man will
travel, where the woman won't. I don't believe this is
fair but the women would be outraged if I told them
it will influence promotion patterns. I'm not going
to tell them of course, but when I'm interviewing for
promotion, it's one of the realities I have to keep in
mind.

If you want to be as promotable as a man, then you should aim
at being as mobile, resilient and available as a man. If achieving
work/life balance is more important to you than a few thousand
extra in your pay cheque or a larger number of people reporting
to you, stay where you are. Ambition should be about exciting
possibilities, not about duty to other women. Never forget the
'Peter Principle,' which holds that most people end up in jobs
that are one promotion past their capabilities. Because they've
performed well at levels one, two and three, they want to get
to level four and management encourage them with favourable
reviews. But in fact, they're a perfect level three person and
should have the courage and the insight to stay put.

If you know you want to be promoted through the ranks,
then set out, each and every day, to be the solution to emerging
problems, rather than the problem. Don't complain about
hassles. Come up with solutions for them. I'm not saying it's
easy for women today, as opposed to the time when Cherie Blair

was twenty-two and a senior figure in British law could get away with saying, in print, that a major barrier to women making it as barristers was that their voices didn't carry as well as male voices did.

But I *am* saying that, first of all, overt discrimination is rare and illegal. Back then, RTÉ had no women newsreaders, because, in a variant of the Cherie Blair quote, it was generally believed that women couldn't 'carry' the news with the authority a man brought to it. Or, more crudely, that viewers would be so fascinated by the clothes a woman wore that they wouldn't be able to concentrate on the news itself. At that time, a group of women led by Gemma Hussey, who later became a Minister for Education, decided to challenge the prejudice about women reading the news. I helped them make a video to hammer home the point, and not long afterwards, women began to appear on radio and TV, reading the news. (I'd love to claim cause and effect, but the fact is that this kind of mindless exclusion was dying on the embarrassed vine everywhere at the time.) And you know what? Although to this day Anne Doyle's jewellery attracts comment, people still manage to understand the content of the news she reads. More to the point, female newscasters have anchored crucially heavy broadcasts. Gráinne Seoige was reading the news on TG4 when the planes went into the Twin Towers, and her colleagues from that time still talk of her endurance in a broadcast which went on for hour after hour. Not only did she present emerging data with confidence and competence, she spent every moment off air handing colleagues New York phone numbers for possible contacts who might add to the story.

It may still be more difficult to get promotion in heavily male organisations but sitting and moaning about it won't solve it. Passivity is not the hallmark of a problem-solver but of a particular corporate pain-in-the-arse who knows they want a management desk, who licks up to the bosses, does the opposite to their own level of employee, argues against the mildest negative observation going into their annual review, applies for every possible promotion and generally paws the ground rather than concentrating on doing what they're currently supposed to be doing. Or who explains away any failure to be promoted by attributing it to the male culture of the place. Be careful about the latter. Sometimes, when you fail to respond to unwritten rules, you cause problems for yourself and everybody else. To go back one final time to Cherie Blair, who, after her husband became British Prime Minister, found herself in a receiving line beside Laura, George Bush's wife. Blair had done this kind of greeting process in Britain and approached it in exactly the same way, chatting to those at the head of the queue. Within minutes, an official voice spoke in her ear.

'Mrs Blair, you're to stop talking to these people,' it told her firmly. 'Just stand here, shake their hands and let the photographer take the picture. That's all they've paid for. We've two hundred and twenty people to get through, so please understand. All they want is their picture with you and the First Lady. Please don't talk to them. That's not the point.'

Did Cherie Blair create a scene, suggesting that whoever designed this process had to be a money-grubbing man who was preventing her deploying her particularly female warmth and ability to connect? No, she didn't. She got the message. A conveyor belt process was going on. Her warbling warmly to some members on the conveyor belt was clogging the works. Professionalism is meeting the specs. She did it.

Some young graduates, entering the workforce, have a frankly unrealistic expectation of how quickly they can reach the top. Fast promotion simply does not happen within some corporate structures. It's no reflection on anybody. If, for example, you go into medicine with the objective of becoming a consultant, it's going to take more than a decade of your life before you can begin to think of achieving your goal. It's not personal. It's just the way that particular profession is structured.

Not all professions have so obvious a stepped process, but checking out the average time taken by someone in your role to get promotion can be wise – it may obviate disappointed expectations. (On the other hand, if you are promoted long before anybody expected you would be, hooray for you. This happened to a young politician named Alan Dukes, later leader of the Fine Gael party, who was appointed Minister for Agriculture on his very first day in Dáil Éireann. It can happen. Grasp it with both hands if it happens to you.)

If you go to work in a small or even a medium-sized company, particularly if it's a family-owned firm, you may find that they don't have formal annual or twice-yearly reviews, as do larger firms and most entities within the civil and public service. They would say they don't need them. If they're not happy with your performance, they'll tell you. If you're not happy with how you're being treated, you'll tell them. After all, you may share the same room or at least the same corridor with them. It's not as if you have to make an appointment to talk to the boss.

This is all fine and dandy if you work for a pretty perfect company. But many people don't. They work for family firms where the family believe nobody outside the family is any good at anything. They work for franchises where obeying the rules and making the numbers is all that counts. They work for exploitative crooks. Or they work for companies which are fine in all the essentials except one. The employer has a neat little niche and a structure that allows them to meet the needs of that niche more or less forever, with reasonable margins. You may get an increase each year that keeps your head above water and your salary above inflation, but that's it. The job carries no promotion prospects because the top guys are not going to retire until they have to.

I have one word for you. Move. Move now, before you start to fester. Move to a new location, a new job. Just don't stay in a position that won't allow you to grow and develop. If you're going to be the same person ten years from now that you are today, you'd better be sure you're happy with that person, including that person's daily occupation. Unless you work part-time, your job is going to take up more of your week than any other occupation except sleeping, and if, in your twenties, you hate waking up in the morning because of the prospect of going to work, then by staying put you are voluntarily submitting yourself to a life-sentence.

The headlines in the newspapers (and, indeed, a later chapter in this book) tend, when they look at negative aspects of the workplace, to focus on bullying and harassment. It's arguable, and the argument is supported by many workplace surveys, that what makes most people unhappy at work is not bullying or harassment. It's boredom and having no control over what you get to do or how you do it. If you're in that kind of a situation, start looking elsewhere. If you are one of those people consultant David Maister calls the 'ones with the shining eyes', you'll find something. And don't hesitate to ask family and friends for help.

If, on the other hand, you work in a company with a coherent personnel development policy and a yearly or six-monthly review, use both. Take any opportunity for training that comes up. Some of it may be complete nonsense – take with a pinch of salt those daft programmes which divide humanity into people with red hats and blue hats and suggest you work out your communication with the world based on these idiotic stereotypes. You'll get something out of even the worst training programme and you'll meet people who may widen your viewpoint on the company and its services or products.

My company trains managers to handle the annual review encounter with individual staff. As a result, we're privy to research within many companies about how the process is seen from either side. That research shows a number of recurring patterns, no matter what the industry or sector the company occupies.

Managers believe:

- They handle difficult reviews well.
- They give negative feedback constructively.
- That feedback is understood and welcomed by the staff member involved.

Time and time again, when the staff member is interviewed about precisely the same encounter, they report that:

- The review was a confusing waste of time.
- They were given nothing but positive feedback.
- They are therefore mystified and infuriated by not immediately receiving promotion or a raise or both.

The disconnect between what the manager intended and what the staff member experienced usually comes about for a simple reason. People don't like to say negative things *to* other people.

In Ireland, we've a genius for saying negative things *about* other people. But up close and personal, it's different. A journalist who has got to know an individual politician, for example, is much less likely to excoriate that politician in print. Once you know someone and like them, you begin to understand why they do what they do in the way they do it. Managers in the feedback situation hope that the recipient of the review will understand what is intended, rather than what is actually articulated.

Never the twain meet, in this kind of session, and the outcomes are markedly worse than directness, in the long term, because trust between boss and subordinate is lost. This is one area where training on both sides is essential. Managers must be able to convey precisely what a staff member is doing right and precisely what they're not yet doing right. Therein lies the crucial assumption of traditionally good management: that, with encouragement, clarity of direction and if necessary further training, the staff member will come up to the mark.

The attitude of traditionally good management matches the attitude of all right-thinking people, who hold that if someone is not behaving correctly, something must be getting in their way. Maybe they lack the skill and could be trained into a better gait of going? Alternatively, maybe they lack insight and can't work out for themselves that arriving an hour late on a Monday morning, so hungover that if someone sneezes, they flinch and take it personally, is not a good career pattern? If so, a good review will sit them down, alert them to their accidental deficits and point them on the road to salvation.

Having for several decades a) managed my own staff on the basis that every one of them had boundless talents and hidden depths; b) advised other managers to do ditto; and c) trained people on the same basis, it came as a great shock to me when the County Manager of Donegal, one Michael McLoone, introduced me to the writings of a counter-intuitive, unorthodox and generally upsetting man named Dr Elliott Jaques. One of the most upsetting factors associated with Elliott Jaques is the English he writes. Reading it is like climbing K2 wearing roller blades. Every time you think you have a grip, you find out painfully how wrong you were.

Dr Jaques does not believe in the infinite perfectibility of human beings. He has little faith in the promotability of most people. His model is a bit like the old army hierarchy. At the bottom, you have the cannon fodder, the lads who have neither the intelligence nor education to take what he calls the 'helicopter view'. They cannot, in other words, no matter how splendidly led, no matter how motivated or diligent they are, ever develop the capacity to think strategically.

This sounds like predestination. It sounds like streaming, which educationalists are against. It sounds like limitation, which the trade unions are against. It sounds elitist, which everybody's against. It sounds like the laying down of arbitrary bounds around the individual's capacity for self-development, career fulfilment and happiness.

Not so. Jaques would maintain that one of the most frustrating issues in modern business is the conviction, on the part of managers and workers alike, that anybody can make it to the top. When someone, despite their own ambition and that of their boss, despite education and training, doesn't get to the next level, they experience bitter frustration. On the other hand, when someone does get to the next level and it then emerges that they have been promoted to the level of their incompetence, it damages the organisation, infuriates those reporting to them and vitiates trust upwards and downwards.

If you plan to get to the top in your own career, read Jaques, because he will widen your understanding of human capacity. Put at its crudest, his theory can be summed up in the old advice against trying to teaching a pig to sing because it will discourage you and irritate the pig.

He also believes that the capacity to think strategically – to take the helicopter view – which is an essential prerequisite of management (or should be) can be measured simply yet scientifically at the first interview. It could be argued that it can be measured simply yet scientifically in secondary school and I personally believe it's inborn and could probably be measured in kindergarten, but I'll come back to that in a minute.

The test Jaques applies is to ask a worker to comment on a controversial question, for example whether or not recreational drugs should be legalised.

The worker will do one of three things:

- They'll flatly declare that legalising bad stuff like marijuana is wrong.
- They'll declare it should be legalised, because prohibition of alcohol was a complete failure in the United States, led to much more drinking and also to people being poisoned or blinded by wood alcohol masquerading as whiskey.
- They'll examine the question from a number of different angles and discuss how each possible action would interact with other possible actions.

Only the third type of person, in the Elliott Jaques model, has the capacity to think and act with a long enough time-frame. Only this person can detach their personal reactions and beliefs from the objective data and the choices to be made thereon. Only this person is developable into a manager and strategic thinker.

The reason I suspect this trait is measurable in quite young children relates to the 'marshmallow test', a psychological experiment done many years ago with kids of about four years of age. They were put in a room with a marshmallow and told that if they didn't eat it, they could have a second when the experimenter came back, fifteen minutes later. They wouldn't be punished for eating the marshmallow except to the extent that if they couldn't hold off, they wouldn't get the extra one.

Some of the children ate the marshmallow immediately: to hell with the second. Some held off. The latter group was capable of what is called 'postponed gratification'. The children had the capacity to imagine what it would be like, within a longer period of time, to eat two marshmallows, rather than get the quick fix of the one in front of them. As they went through childhood and adolescence, the children in the marshmallow test continued to be monitored and it emerged that the ones capable of postponed gratification were more successful in exams, in careers and in life.

While nobody suggests it's possible to identify the future CEO of AIB while they're in the playgroup, what is clear is that certain traits, established early in life, can greatly influence an individual's later capacity for such a top job.

The difficulty is that, almost from birth, we are told to aim high. Anyone who does an MBA or an MSc reads case study after case study while also consuming business books about or by the people who aimed high and got there. Although women are rarely pushed in the way men are pushed, they are nonetheless not immune to the belief that if they work hard, they can make it right to the top, and they become thwarted and bitter if it doesn't happen.

The first indication that it may not happen is the review which manages to be positive, but not positive enough. Managers should be able to say, 'Antoinette, you are the ultimate project manager. You brought in that new product with every 'i' dotted and 't' crossed. You brought it in slightly ahead of time. Now, I know you want to be considered for the vice-presidency of production, but it would make no corporate sense to put you in that position. It would call for characteristics you don't have and would find it impossible to develop. Where we need you is in project management, so we're raising your salary as well as giving you a bonus.'

However, this rarely if ever happens, because of the overriding imperative to promote, promote, promote. Some multinationals even have an 'up or out' philosophy, because they do not like to have someone at some point in the hierarchy whose onward progress has stopped. Why? If an executive is perfect for a role one year, whence comes the belief that they will become gangrenous five years later?

If you're working in this kind of company and don't want to take the extra stress overseas experience or promotion to a higher level would bring, you may find yourself in an untenable position. Or, if you play it right, the person you report to will find you so useful to them that they will manage to conceal you in the undergrowth. The key to a happy career is always to be the solution to someone's problem, never to be the problem.

Which brings us to the review which you figure is going to stall your upward progress and lay down a marker about your limitations. You may have a sense that it's coming, because of last year's review or because of small comments made throughout the year by the manager you report to, or because, in some companies, a draft review is sent to the executive a week or so in advance of the conversation with their manager.

Before you go into any review meeting, have the meeting with yourself. Be honest about how you have performed during the previous year. No excuses. Be equally honest about what you want in the coming year. What you want. Not what your boss wants, or your partner wants, or your pals want. What you want. A review meeting is a negotiation. More than five centuries ago, Francis Bacon wrote an essay, 'Of Negociating', in which he stressed the need, in advance of any such meeting, to prepare for it in the light of what you know about the individual on the other side of the table:

> If you would work any man, you must either know his nature and fashions, and so lead him; or his ends, and so persuade him; or his weakness and disadvantages, and so awe him; or those that have interest in him, and so govern him. In dealing with cunning persons, we must ever consider their ends, to interpret their speeches; and it is good to say little to them, and that which they least look for. In all negociations of difficulty, a man may not look to sow and reap at once; but must prepare business, and so ripen it by degrees.

Relevant to a review meeting in the twenty-first century? Absolutely.

Bacon's point about knowing the nature of the person on the other side of the negotiation is particularly relevant to women. Popularly attributed to the fact that women are more in touch with the right side of their brain than men, females have a tendency to deal in impressions, feelings and anecdotes, whereas men have a tendency to deal in facts, objectives and structures. Like all generalities, this one is full of holes, but let's assume you're working for a man who (you would say in your sourer moments) 'plays the system', 'talks the talk', and 'thinks in corporate-speak'.

At the review, he indicates that you have certain deficits when it comes to team-working, goal-focus and communication. You sit in front of him, a raging blush rising from your chest to your face, tears sparking in your eyes and tell him you feel you're a great team-member and communicator and you can't imagine why he'd think you're not goal-focused, given that you worked six weekends in a row to make sure a particular report got out on time.

He gently points out that you shouldn't have had to work those weekends but that because you didn't delegate any of the tasks inherent in the report, you ended up doing it all yourself. You sit there feeling unappreciated, wounded and disregarded.

You come out afterwards and tell some of your female colleagues about it. They tell you he's a soulless shit, that it's a disgrace you're not getting promoted and – if you start to blub – tell you it's all right to cry.

It isn't. In one large commercial firm I've consulted with, if you mention crying at work, everybody immediately talks about the senior woman who cried in front of a client. It's ten years ago, and she left the company within months of the tearful episode but it still freaks them out. It's never productive to cry at work and if you have a tendency to do so, remove yourself from the company of others whenever tears threaten. Crying at work is seen by most male managers and a substantial number of female managers as inadequacy or manipulation. They may yield to it but it's got no place in your armoury of communication if you want to be seen as a calmly confident professional.

The first rule of office negotiation was articulated by one of the gentlest men I know. Dermot McCrum, now CEO of the Drama Academy Development Company, backed by the Cathal Ryan Trust, once had a meeting with a subordinate who had produced a video a client had rejected. The video producer was wounded to the core and said so. At length, he said so. He said his feelings were hurt. He said he'd never expected any client to go behind his back to the boss (Dermot being the boss). He said he felt he'd been betrayed and traduced.

Dermot listened patiently to all this and then took charge of the meeting. 'Now, putting your feelings to one side,' he began.

The employee with whom he was dealing almost lost his reason. Put his feelings to one side? Yes, Dermot said equably. It was now time to deal with the realities. And deal with the realities the two of them did, to the client's eventual satisfaction. Among Dermot's colleagues, though, the phrase took on the flavour of legend. One of us would give out stink about someone.

'Now, putting your feelings to one side,' someone else would prompt, and the person doing the venting would swear, laugh and get back to the business, as opposed to the emotional self-expression.

Feelings have no place in an annual review. Having decided in advance what you want to achieve, you then work out how to achieve it. What evidence can you produce, for example, to justify a claim that you've rectified any deficits adduced at the last review? It doesn't matter that you may feel you've improved as a listener. Without evidence, the claim is without merit.

The same applies to your opposite number in the meeting.

If he or she has decided you're the best thing since the crispy baguette, that you're clever, dedicated, insightful, innovative, creative, supportive, brilliant at meeting deadlines and likely to be the next president of the company if not the country, and if that's what they're going to put in the report that will go into your Human Resources file, I wouldn't push them for evidence. You're playing a blinder, so keep your head down and look modestly pleased.

If, however, the boss across the table is unsatisfied with your performance, don't let them away with general statements like:

- We have an issue with your punctuality.
- You're not the best team player.
- As a communicator, you leave a lot to be desired.

Ask for specific instances. Now, this needs to be caveated up to the gills. If you know you never arrive on time and that members of your team have taken to sending you e-mails because they trust you so little, face-to-face, then maybe it's not a great idea to ask the boss to produce examples of the alleged wrongdoing, because they may give you a list as long as a bus timetable. Being asked for it may make them remember more examples than they would otherwise recall of you arriving for a breakfast meeting mid-afternoon.

However, if you wish to challenge any negative conclusion being reached, you are entitled to ask for evidence, not assertion, and your boss, if he or she is any good at their job, will be able to provide you with that evidence. If they're unprepared for the meeting, they will follow the law of recency, listing the late you had last week. In which case you are entitled to point out that just as one swallow doesn't constitute a summer, neither does one late establish unpunctuality.

Keep your voice at an even level, don't whinge, and don't introduce any of your requests for exemplification with negative phraseology.

'But if you think I'm so lacking in communications skills, you should be able to give me examples that would justify what you're saying,' is somewhere between a reproach and a declaration of war.

'On the communications skills issue, maybe you could help me with an example so I have a clear sense of it?' is much more positive.

If a positive response induces the boss to back off and say it's really not that serious, be gently persistent: if he or she has observed something they want you to improve, you want to work on it, so an example would help...Of course, if an example isn't forthcoming, you can gently and positively bat the allegation out of court.

'I appreciate that communication is important,' you say, 'and I'm really happy you find my communication skills up to scratch. Now, about the time-keeping...'

Your overall objective may be promotion, a bonus, a salary increase or all three. Your interim objective – a step along the road to the main objective – is to ensure that nothing negative goes in writing on your personnel file. The fact that your boss may have an impression of you as surly, secretive and seditious is beside the point. That impression could be based on backstairs gossip. But just as hearsay wouldn't stand up in court, it has no place in a yearly review. (You'd be well advised, however, if you know the impression is rooted in reality, to buck up your time-keeping or whatever is at the heart of the bad impression, because your boss is going to learn from your requests for evidence and next time around, will have that evidence for you. In bucketfuls, if you don't mend your ways.)

When you enter the room where the review is to take place, make sure you have a folder or a pad with you, with some headings already written down. This isn't a teacher-pupil encounter where the teacher (the boss) gives you (the pupil) the results of an exam. It's a discussion to which both sides bring topics, the conclusion of which should be influenced by both participants.

If you think there's a chance you're not going to be fairly dealt with, the presence of your pad and pen may be the best thing you have going for you. Three years ago, I prepared a middle manager in a big marketing organisation for her review. She had gone to work for an exacting yet warmly paternal man, who had been particularly kind to her when her father, whom she adored, died suddenly. When she got engaged, six months after her father's death, her boss's attitude towards her changed. Instead of handing her projects and responding positively when she presented the completed work, he started hounding her, demanding to know if she had completed this detail or that detail and, at the last review, had told her he was extremely disappointed in her and that she was an uncreative weight around the neck of his department.

When she came to me, she was distraught, going over and over in her mind all the possible reasons for him to have 'gone off her'.

'I wonder if it was that he thought of me as younger and more dependent on him than I am?' she speculated. 'He treated me sort of as a daughter – an adopted daughter – while I was grieving my dad. D'you think it's possible that my getting engaged forced him to realise that I was grown up and that he was my boss, not some kind of semi-paternal support figure, and that upset him?'

'Who cares?' I asked.

'Well, it must be something,' she said.

'Is this stuff about him seeing you as an adopted daughter going to appear on your file when he gives you a godawful review next week?'

She shook her head silently.

'Did any of it appear in last year's godawful review?'

Another headshake, this time with blinks that clumped her eyelashes wetly together.

'You have limited time,' I told her, ignoring the tears. 'Your review is six days away. If he gives you one like last year, your chances of the promotion you want are straight down the tubes. You don't have the time to be doing sympathetic amateur psychoanalysis on this guy.'

(I thought, by the way, she was probably correct. This woman was twenty-six but looked five years younger.)

'This is about me, not about him, right?'

'Precisely.'

She thought about this for a moment, her forefinger patting her coral-pink lower lip, then straightened up, ready for business.

'Fuck him,' she said with great precision.

That was so unexpected that it made me laugh and my laughter infected her in turn. Then she became very serious.

'He'll make me cry,' she said. 'And I'll have to ask him to terminate the meeting early and agree to what he says he's putting on my file.'

'Remind me what it was you said a minute ago?'

She rewound her mental tape and looked puzzled.

'D'you mean "fuck him"?'

'You're not going to cry, because the first time he makes one of his big sweeping condemnations –'

'"I have to tell you – and it's with great regret I have to tell you – that in all my years in this firm, I have yet to be so grievously disappointed by any staff member as I have been by you…"'

'Right. The first time he does that speech, you take the cap off your pen and sit poised. When he hits a full stop, you ask him for specific examples of specific behaviours that have led him to develop this impression of you.'

'He'll say it's not an impression.'

'Good, in that case he'll have no problems coming up with the data that you will faithfully write down.'

'Say if he asks me what I'm writing?'

'Say if he does?'

'What do I say?'

'What's the truth?'

'If I'm doing anything that isn't professional, I want to fix it.'

'And?'

'And what?'

I gestured towards her pad and pen.

'Oh, right. And that's why I'm making notes of the things he wants me to fix.'

She went into the review meeting clutching that pen and pad like life-preservers. But because she's hyper-aware of other people's gaze patterns (as good actors are and good therapists also) she realised that he was seriously put out by her new props. Particularly when he couldn't get to the right angle to read what she had already written on the front page. And even more so when she started to make notes of his accusations. Within minutes, he found an excuse to abandon the procedure and get sign-off from her to a positive review which just coincidentally opened up a post for her in another division, far, far away from his influence.

'Seems rather a big consequence to arise out of one pad and pen,' I said, when she came back for a cup of coffee to celebrate her promotion.

'Well, I have a theory,' she announced. 'But you probably don't want me wasting time psychoanalysing him.'

'Go for it.'

'I think the minute I laid out the pad and took the cap off the pen very carefully, like so –' she demonstrated ' – he immediately knew this was a new me. This is a clever man, and I think he figured I'd taken advice. The only mistake he made was I think he decided I'd taken legal advice and was making notes to produce in a constructive dismissal case or a bullying case and he just panicked and wanted me and my note-taking out of there as fast as humanly possible.'

'And I presume you felt the same way?'

'Sorry?'

'You also wanted the meeting to end as soon as possible?'

She laughed and began to flip through the earlier pages on her pad.

'No,' she said. 'I was having a great time. I was making these notes for myself and writing them terribly tiny so he couldn't read them. It was driving him nuts.'

She found the page she was looking for and twirled it so I could read the neat phrases in perfect handwriting: cowardy cowardy custard you can't give me a reason. cowardy cowardy custard you thought I'd cry, didn't you? cowardy cowardy custard...

If you're making notes in a review, it might be tempting to do as she did. But you don't have as good a reason. And you might have a need for accurate recording of what went on in the review meeting.

Because it may represent a key step on the road to achieving your overall ambition.

But that's when you get into problems caused by other people. Most of the problems that prevent women from being promoted are self-created.

TEN WAYS WOMEN OBSTRUCT THEIR OWN PROMOTIONS

1. They don't problem-solve
2. They're tedious about their lover, their weight, their cat, their skincare or how much work they have to do (which is never as much as they think it is).
3. They create a grotty office, leaving jackets over the back of chairs, empty coffee cups everywhere and a handbag the size of a small skip on their desk.
4. They don't remind the man or woman they report to of tasks to be completed. (The boss is nearly always busier on a wider range of issues than the junior. Keep them right and you'll keep yourself right.)
5. They send e-mails rather than getting off their arses and going to talk to people.
6. They do the least they can get away with, not the most they can contribute.
7. They never take the blame, but always take the credit.
8. They never work through lunch, take long cigarette-breaks and have no sense of urgency.
9. They're indiscreet.
10. They've no emotional intelligence, so they raise gripes with the boss when the boss is going down for the third

time under problems that are bigger and more immediate than theirs are.

11

WOMEN IN MANAGEMENT

'Sir, a woman preaching is like a dog's walking on his hind legs. It is not done well; but you are surprised to find it done at all...'

Samuel Johnson

'It's easier for a man in my position to pick up the phone to his customer and organise a golfing day or whatever...there is an advantage there.'

'I don't play golf therefore am not visible and you would feel under pressure to pick it up.'

Two women speaking. Two middle managers, quoted in a study designed to further our understanding of the barriers faced by women trying to get to the top. The study, by Christine Cross, a lecturer in the University of Limerick, is one of several examining the problems of businesswomen included in the 2005 edition of *The Irish Business Journal*, issued by the Cork Institute of Technology. Cross writes:

> Despite the rapid increase in female participation in the paid labour-force across the globe, considerable evidence has been gathered that documents a scarcity

of women in executive level positions. Since the 1970s female participation in the Irish labour force has grown from 28 percent at the start of the 1970s to over fifty percent in 2001…despite this unprecedented growth, a recent Irish report conducted by the Irish Business and Employers Confederation (IBEC) highlights that the gender gap remains a significant feature of organisational life in Ireland, with only 8 per cent of chief executives and 21 per cent of senior managers being female.

The study specifically examines two possible contributors to the 'glass ceiling' inhibiting women's upward mobility in business. Those two factors are reconciling work and family conflict and networking.

The first of these surfaces constantly. Any reasonably successful woman in business or politics with a partner and offspring inevitably finds herself asked the 'How do you balance work and family commitments?' question. The answer, for a woman who believes in equality, is: 'Of how many men have you asked that question?' because if we claim equality, then we shouldn't answer questions that assume we buy into inequality and assume, into the bargain, that nothing has happened in the last thirty years to the traditional roles of men and women.

Once you relinquish the concept of equal responsibilities, you're on the slide right back to the feminine mystique and in no time at all are agreeing to share your recipes for Christmas pudding and be photographed in the kitchen.

Their willingness or lack thereof to leave their own kitchen is one of the most ignored factors in women's failure to make it to the top ranks. One woman who *has* made it to top management in one of our biggest state-sponsored bodies told me this week that she has no doubt her progress was aided by her willingness to do off-site work when asked:

> Of course management make a judgment when a woman says she can't take on a trip. They make the judgment that the woman and her partner don't see the woman's career as being as important as the man's. It's a perfectly legitimate judgment to make. Because if their careers are equal and their responsibilities to their children are equal, then it's up to them, as a couple, to manage the issue in a way that doesn't diminish the woman's contribution to her employing organisation. More importantly, conferences, seminars and other off-site tasks are golden opportunities for networking and if you don't take those opportunities you are, effectively, choosing to move on to the slow track in terms of promotion.

Her comment brings into sharp relief the popular – and shallow – perception of 'networking'. Networking for women tends to be presented as an issue of business-card swopping. You measure your networking success in any given week by how many cards you've given or received, giving yourself bonus points if you've managed to write a personal observation about the card-giver on the card.

This is matched in popularity by the notion that women's progress to the top is halted by their inability to drop everything, grab a golf-bag and bond with colleagues on the third tee. The fact that a lot of women believe this doesn't mean it's true. A lot of us believe that the bad news delivered by the bathroom scales this morning is caused by us having big bones, but if we believe it too strongly, we'll find ourselves wearing size 18 suits as our bones get bigger and bigger.

Women who really want to make it to the top generally do so, if they have the competence. Women who only *think* they want to make it to the top (or have unowned ambition wished on them by someone else) generally don't do so, despite their competence, but at least have the comfort of popular explanations including the golf-as-exclusion-methodology one, the childcare-deficit one, the stereotyping one and the office politics.

That said, it has to be acknowledged that although women are getting to the top in slowly increasing numbers, the *New York Times* worked out that, because, even though the picture has improved, so few women make it to leadership positions in politics, public life or business that it will take 270 years before absolute equality of representation is achieved.

If you're one of the ones who slide through the glass ceiling and make it to the top, you want to make the best of your time there. Not as a woman. As a manager or leader.

Just as women are judged differently at every stage in their career, they are judged differently when they reach the top. Media profiles and interviews are qualitatively different – if the woman manager allows them to be – in their level of attention to husbands/partners and children. Expectations are also different, not least on the part of women, many of whom believe that a top female manager should bring the qualities they associate with womanhood into play. They want women in management to have a quite different style to that of men. To be more consultative, less directive. Warmer and gentler, less abrasive.

On the other side of that coin is research which suggests that the more women in top management behave like an aggressive man, the more they tend to be respected as leaders. It's a contradiction no woman in management can afford to waste time on. Once you've got to the top, your style is already established and you should get on with it as best you can.

Making the transition to top management, at least in theory, is easier if you move businesses at the same time as you change roles. That way, you don't have to compete with your own past and achieve the transition in relationships required by your upward progress. It doesn't always work, though. Carly Fiorina, former President of Hewlett Packard, was head-hunted for the prestigious post. She had previously headed a company called Lucent. She brought from Lucent an enviable track record, a charismatic personality and a husband who had retired in order to be her support system.

Most women in management would envy that last bit. But the combination didn't work. Fiorina infuriated the major shareholders of HP, failed to read the intent of the board and was out on her ear despite orchestrating the merger with Compaq, which enthralled the business pages while it was going on. Her memoir of those years is poignant and instructive. Particularly about the unique challenges facing the woman who makes it to the top in traditionally male hierarchies.

One of those challenges is communication. Women are great communicators. They're masters of anecdote and of illustration. But, according to one communications analyst, that's not enough, when a woman gets to the top.

'Women are relative strangers to senior management and most have underestimated the threat their presence poses to the set of comfortable communication patterns men have developed – the "language" that ultimately separates leaders from non-leaders,' says Kathleen Kelley Reardon in *They Don't Get it, Do*

They? (Little, Brown, 1995)

I've dealt with the language that separates leaders from non-leaders in an earlier book, *Talk the Talk*. But here are a few pointers:

- Women apologise for themselves. Men don't.
- Women express feelings and personal convictions. Men express data and conclusions.
- Women modify what they say. Men state and only then qualify.
- Women use small no-harm-in-me phrases like 'just.' ('I'd just like to raise an issue here about diversity...') Men don't.
- Women attribute their own success to luck. Men attribute their own success to their own intelligence and hard work.
- Women sulk. Men yell.

Of course those are sexist generalities and don't apply to you. Congratulations. But they're also realities, observed over twenty years of working with women. And observed by women who have made it to the top, internationally. According to Madeleine Albright, the former US Secretary of State, one of the big disadvantages women have is a tentativeness which is either inborn or developed through their education:

> One thing that happens to every woman – no matter where she is – is that she goes to a meeting, listens, and then thinks that she might want to make a point. But then she doubts herself and worries that what she wants to say is not really smart, so she decides

not to say anything. And then some man says exactly what she was going to say, and everyone thinks it's brilliant. Then the woman wishes she had spoken. I had my first experience with this when I first went to an informal session of the Security Council. I thought to myself, 'I'll just wait and see who's who, and try to get a sense of the personalities and dynamics in the room before I speak.' And then it occurred to me, 'I can't do that! I'm the United States, I have to speak or our view will not be evident.' That was the first time I realised that as a woman, you often have to separate the way that you might feel as a woman from what your responsibilities are as a leader. I also learned that you have to adapt to the fact that the adjectives applied to men and women are different. If a woman really cares about something, she's called 'emotional', but a man can be called 'passionate'. So I think I learned to argue in a way that was calmer, in a way that did not expose my deep feelings about an issue.

Women in top management should never cease listening. Nor should they set out to make a point for the sake of making a point. But if you want to achieve an end result, your communication must be geared to do just that. Which requires planning, phrasing and determined intervention, so that those present at a meeting hear what you've said, register it as important, are persuaded by it and act differently as a result of it. That's leadership. That's management.

And, lest we forget, women may not consciously or deliberately be discriminated against but if they're not making it to the top in the numbers we might expect, something's preventing them. Tipping the balance just a little the other way is within the power of the few women who do make it to the top. Madeline Albright puts it this way:

> There is a special place in hell for women who don't help each other. A woman with power must understand that, in actuality, her role is to help others. For a woman who wants to be at the centre of power, she must understand that her power is actually maximised by encouraging more women to participate in the system.

12

The Fame Game

My best assets have been acting and just being pleasant...

Sally Field

There she was in the Rolls, clutching her flute of champagne. Fabulously glamorous. Household name. Chuffed with her own event-management. A girl at the top of her game. A few weeks later, Katy French was dead from heart failure believed to have resulted from cocaine.

The problem is the nature of the game. The fame-without-competence game. God love her, she has now given her name to it. Branded it. Katy French fame. That how it's going to be known, from now on.

It's the kind of fame based on luck and looks. It blazes with arc-light brightness – for a short time. It lights up the owner in photographs at parties. On reality TV shows. At public events. It's all about adrenalin, excitement and hanging around with other celebs.

The first time I registered a new hunger for fame, *per se,* among young women was when I did a lecture on a university course for aspiring journalists. When the lecture was over, I found myself surrounded by nineteen- and twenty-years-olds who didn't look the way students looked when I was their age. They were glamorous, made up, groomed and possessed enviable shoes. What they wanted from me was guidance on how to get into TV.

'As what?' I asked.

They collectively shrugged. As anything, was the message of the shrugs.

'But what do you want to be?'

Another set of shrugs.

'Famous?' one of them eventually suggested.

'Just famous?'

Nods, this time, instead of shrugs.

'But d'you want to read the news or be Miriam O'Callaghan on *Prime Time* or be a legal affairs correspondent or...?'

We were back to the shrugs. These marvellously confident students were: a) convinced that they could do any of the above; and b) didn't much care. Any of the professional endeavours listed would serve as a vehicle to take them where they wanted to be, which was famous.

Fame has always been the spur but it's usually been an instrument to achieve something else. Now it's an objective in and of itself. And appearing on reality TV programmes is one of the ways some businesswomen think they can achieve it.

It's good for my business. Increasingly, the Communications Clinic gets contacted by companies which want to figure in an episode of such a programme, by individuals who have been invited to take part and by eager young women who have already committed themselves to a series.

Of the three, the first is the easiest and most productive option. If you have an attractive premises, an interesting product or service and can unselfconsciously engage on camera with apprentices undertaking some kind of project, it's possible to get good PR out of involving your company in a reality TV programme. In the beginning, such involvement came for free. Now you can expect it to set you back a lot of money. When companies come to us asking our advice on this as a proposition, they usually do so after they've committed themselves, at which point there's no gain in suggesting that they could have got themselves a highly effective radio ad campaign for the same price. They are seduced by TV and by fame, just as much as the students I met were seduced by them.

The second way people get onto reality TV is by being marginally or historically famous or notorious. (Join the dots yourself.) The wise ones smile and refuse the invitation. The others accept, hoping to reinvent themselves, to move from the C-celeb list to the B-list or revive a moribund career. And convince themselves that the real reason they're doing it is to earn money for their favourite charity.

Then there are the thousands of mostly young people, many of them female, who apply, compete, undergo psychological testing, take time off work and submit themselves to several weeks of physical stress, emotional pressure and public humiliation. When you ask them what possessed them to even consider such a career move, they tell you they have the chance of a €100K-a-year job working with a household name and that would be much more exciting than their current job. That, of course, is if they win. The odds are heavily stacked against their winning, but, just as shoppers buy Lottery tickets every week, knowing, because the odds of winning are printed on the ticket, how small are their chances of taking home the jackpot, women who enter the reality TV arena hope against hope that they'll be the one to get through and become a national success story.

The overwhelming majority of the participants in any reality TV programme vanish without trace within a year. The exceptions either have some talent (like Anna Nolan, who ended up presenting several RTÉ programmes) or a Panzer-like determination.

If you're a smart young businesswoman who figures participating in an apprentice-type programme would give your career a hell of a boost, be careful. One of the reasons the production companies spend so much time selecting the participants is to provide mutual contention: they set up one kind of personality against another kind and wait for the sparks to fly while the camera observes. The thoughtful analyst of a situation doesn't come well out of this kind of programme: quiet reflection is a pain in the ass from an entertainment point of view. Once in the situation, divorced from all your normal frames of reference, you operate at a level of heightened emotional tension which may cause you to say or do things that will do your career no good in the longer term.

If, on the other hand, you just want to be famous, go right ahead. Be the latest iteration of Kerry Katona. Just be aware that there's always another, younger more glamorous girl coming along behind. Another girl who's prepared to be more outrageous, more profane, more willing to feed the fame animal.

If you're famous because you have a skill, that fame tends to last. You can even buzz off for a few years, be out of the spotlight – like Bibi Baskin – and then come back and use your skill again. Because you're not famous simply for being famous. You're famous for your interviewing skills. Or your writing skills. Or your singing. Or your dancing. You get through the minefield, sufficiently insulated by your skill so that, when the media in general or one media outlet in particular turn against you, you survive the blast.

Without skill, without competence, fame is achievable but hugely dangerous. It's like keeping a tiger cub as a pet. Dead easy in the beginning. But as the animal grows, it needs more feeding, and patting it on the head becomes increasingly risky.

Feeding the media beast requires constant self-reinvention. That's possible if you have a core skill. Madonna has demonstrated it better than anyone. She does whatever it takes, from sugarloaf cone bras to pretend lesbian kisses. But the woman can sing.

Absent a skill or talent, the owner of fame has limited capacity to reinvent themselves, other than by gutting their private lives and acting in increasingly wild and crazy ways. It works, in the short term.

In the longer term, it becomes a bore. The cameras move elsewhere, the gossip columnists find another hottie. And, too frequently, the fame-seeker is left with an addiction, a habit that can't be maintained.

The classic example of this kind of addiction, this endless lust simply to be famous at all costs, is Monica Lewinsky. The American journalist Maureen Orth has written about meeting Lewinsky by accident at a social event in Washington:

> When she heard I was with *Vanity Fair*, it became clear she wanted to be photographed for the magazine. Her eagerness to be immortalised in this once-humiliating situation suggested that – like her lawyer at the time – she had acquired a case of advanced attention addiction. Like so many, Lewinsky had lost any sense of the distinction between fame and infamy.

There's the rub. The distinction between fame and infamy is now dangerously eroded. There's a premium on notoriety, no matter how it's earned. Many clever and skilful people, down the centuries, have worked hard, not only at their trade but at being famous. Madame Tussaud parlayed her stories of being around as the guillotine carved off royal heads into a brand which still carries clout. German playwright Schiller described the public as 'my preoccupation, my sovereign and my friend…' Norman Mailer never encountered a microphone without wanting to talk to it. But for each of them, fame had a purpose and was justified by their work. Now, drug-addiction, self-mutilation and eating disorders all deliver fame. Of a sort.

The blurring of the line between fame and infamy creates a context complicated by the speed of churn. A couple of decades back, the cycle of build-'em-up-now-tear-'em-down took a long time. Now, thanks to the availability of a celeb's every syllable on the Web, the cycle is shockingly fast.

The real tragedy of Katy French Fame is that it happens to young people at a time in their life when they believe themselves immortal and impregnable. Sometimes they survive it. Sometimes it kills them.

And when it kills them, there's no perpetrator. Media shrug and moves on.

Because that's the nature of the media beast.

13

Bullying and Harassment

> *Harassment is any form of unwanted conduct re-*
> *lated to any of the discriminatory grounds, and*
> *sexual harassment is any form of unwanted verbal,*
> *non-verbal or physical conduct of a sexual nature,*
> *being conduct which in either case has the purpose*
> *or effect of violating a person's dignity and creating*
> *an intimidating, hostile, degrading, humiliating or*
> *offensive environment for the person.*
>
> *Such unwanted conduct may consist of acts, requests,*
> *spoken words, gestures or the production, display*
> *or circulation of written words, pictures or other*
> *material.*
>
> Employment Equality Acts, 1998-2007

Workplace bullying is defined as follows in the Health and Safety Authority and Labour Relations Commission Codes of Practice.

> Workplace bullying is repeated inappropriate be-
> haviour, direct or indirect, whether verbal, physical or
> otherwise conducted by one or more persons against

another or others, at the place of work and/or in the course of employment, which could reasonably be regarded as undermining the individual's right to dignity at work. An isolated incident of the behaviour described in this definition may be an affront to dignity at work but as a once-off incident is not considered to be bullying.

Every year, women make complaints to their employers of sexual harassment or bullying. And perhaps three times as many women who believe they have been sexually harassed or bullied do nothing about it. They don't go the complaint route, in some cases because they fear that nobody would believe their side of the story or they would have to resign from their current jobs and would have difficulty explaining to a potential new employer the circumstances which caused their career move.

Every year, some employers on the receiving end of those complaints are: a) astonished when they first learn about the case; b) convinced that the woman is going to lose, because what they, the employer did or allowed to happen was perfectly normal; c) shattered by the publicity attendant upon the case; and d) devastated when they discover that they may have a liability.

Let's look at two different – and heavily fictionalised – examples.

COMPANY A

Mid-sized operation, less than fifteen years old. Set up by a bunch of electronics engineers who were school and college pals. The company grew faster than any of them expected, and attracted lots of new employees. In the early stages, the new hires were drawn in by contacts: one of the guys would mention to a friend their need for an employee in a particular area and recruit the man or woman recommended by the friend. After a while, the friends-of-friends pipeline dried up, so they hired people by interview.

Company A operated casually. Casual in dress. Casual in attitude. Casual in behaviour. Lots of mutual abuse by lads as a method of expressing mutual affection. Lots of comments on the boob-size and legs of the girls. Lots of speculation on a Monday as to who scored over the weekend. Everybody having a great time. Or so the bosses thought. Until they were hit by a complaint from one of the newer female employees. They thought – and said among themselves on e-mail – that she was a prissy cow and they should never have hired her. They told her to get a grip. She went legal. They lost.

COMPANY B

A slightly smaller, older company with a much quieter, more respectful culture, that culture driven by a managing director who was gentle by nature and conflict-avoidant. Both traits caused him problems when one of the newer women turned out to be – as the rest of the employees felt – lazy and time-wasting, particularly at meetings. He made a couple of interventions, which the rest of the staff thought far too soft.

'Leave her alone, she'll come round,' he told them. They doubted that she would 'come round', but went along with his direction, leaving her out of meetings to minimise conflict and hassle. When she asked for details about the company's grievance policy, the MD was astonished. Grievance policy? Yes, she told him. You're supposed to have one.

His PA looked up grievance policies on the Internet and downloaded one of them.

'That looks OK,' he said. 'Shove the company name on it and give her a copy.'

Shortly afterwards, he received a letter of complaint which clearly had been informed by legal advice, claiming bullying and exclusion and listing the meetings from which the employee had been excluded. The MD gathered his management around him to consider this missive. Once the collective rage died down, someone got to the point.

'Either we include her and go back to where we were, or we get sued.'

The group silently considered these options.

'No bloody way,' someone said.

'You want to get sued?' someone else asked.

'We need legal advice,' a third offered.

They got legal advice and met again. At that meeting, the consensus was that it had been a mistake to hire this employee and that the best thing to do – lawyer to lawyer – was to agree a mechanism of parting. It cost the small company half its projected profits for the year.

What both cases illustrate is that bullying and harassment are, to use layperson's terms, in the eye of the beholder. What matters is not how the company or boss or colleagues see the issue. What matters is how the individual perceives themselves to have been treated.

In legal terms, here's how it works. Basic standards of behaviour are required while you are at your workplace. Each employee should be free to determine what is acceptable to him/her. This right should not be undermined by the fact that the perpetrator, or indeed other colleagues, may consider the offending behaviour acceptable.

Company A had a number of problems. First of all, it assumed that the way its people behaved among themselves would be found acceptable by everybody coming into the company. It ignored the fact that the employer had legal obligations towards its employees to provide a safe place of work and an environment free of bullying and harassment and in which the dignity of everyone is respected and also the fact that the employee had legal rights. Secondly, it reacted stupidly. Its people exacerbated the issue by communicating badly with the complainant and by communicating with each other by e-mail in terms which made the case much worse. Not only did it lose money as a result: it lost reputation because of the publicity which resulted.

Company B didn't understand that bullying doesn't have to consist of yelling and threatening behaviour. Simply leaving someone out of communications or meetings can be interpreted as exclusion. They avoided reputation-damage by settling with the complainant and learned a series of lessons:

- They should have had a better system of feedback.
- They should have had an effective code of conduct or grievance-process, understood by managers and employees alike, which regulated the conduct of employees in the workplace and included policies and procedures dealing with bullying and sexual harassment.
- They needed to look at their recruitment and review processes.

If you believe you're being bullied or harassed or excluded, the first thing to do is neither legal nor procedural. It's personal. Sometimes, when women feel they're in this position, the problem is just that: they feel it. And they feel that the other person or people involved should know that they feel it.

There's no 'shoulds' in real life. Before you decide what to do about your predicament , sit down and ask yourself some blunt questions:

1. What happened?
2. How often has it happened? Was there a pattern?
3. When did it happen? When does it tend to happen?
4. Where did it/does it happen?
5. Who did it/does it?
6. Why does it bother me?
7. Is there a code of conduct? If so, does it deal with the misconduct?
8. Do I need to seek professional advice?

WHAT HAPPENED?

Over the past decade, I've been consulted by executives making a number of complaints about what happened to them in their workplace.

- One male executive was told, just before a concert sponsored by his employer, that 'it wouldn't be a good idea' to bring his (male) partner to the event. 'We're not that kind of company,' his colleague told him.
- A woman who'd served as PA to the CEO of a major state-sponsored body got a new boss. He was popular, liked and dynamic. He improved her pay. And every time he passed her desk, he touched her. Sometimes it was an affectionate hug. Sometimes he patted her on the back. Now and then

he did an impromptu neck massage.

- An accountant who had been with a company for six months found, at the Christmas party, that she was expected to take part in a quiz with jokey questions based on the sexual behaviours of herself and her colleagues.

- A technical writer's boss, when he perceived her work was not up to scratch, tore the hard copy of it up in public and tossed it in the air.

- A new recruit received e-mails complimenting her on the shortness of her skirts.

- A sign in one office occupied by three young women and one fifty-five year old woman read: 'No Tears. No whinges. No pregnancies.'

- At coffee breaks in her company, a Jewish executive found herself listening to jokes about rabbis.

- A twenty-two-year-old embarked on a relationship with a boss who told her he was separated from his wife. After a few months, her predecessor in the job rang her and suggested a cup of coffee in Starbucks, over which she explained that the flat to which her boss was bringing her was not his home – just his location for serial infidelity to a wife to whom he was still very much married. Her predecessor had also been involved with the man. The twenty-two-year-old terminated the relationship, only to find her former lover sending subtle signals that she was not up to the job: sighs when she indicated she wanted to speak at meetings and small 'what was that about?' pauses when she finished.

- A single mother was referred to – humorously – as a 'Ho.'

Here are examples of the different ways some of these people responded. The man who had been told, ostensibly by a pal with his best interests at heart, not to bring his partner of fifteen years to company events, was deeply offended by the advice and by the corporate culture underlying that advice. He decided not to challenge the management at the time, for personal reasons. His mother had recently died, after a long illness. He had left his last job to nurse her, so had a gap in his CV. If he then left his new, highly paid and extremely prestigious job or got involved in litigation, he believed it would gravely damage his career path. He discussed it with his partner.

'Those company events happen – what? – every six months?' was his partner's response. 'My life's not gonna be blighted by being excluded from a gathering of people I'd hate anyway. You go. If necessary, bring one of the girls who doesn't currently have a fella. Make a bit of money and get the hell out in two years.'

The woman being mauled (as she saw it) by her boss got an older colleague to point out quietly to him that he was endangering his own position by so much touching. He was shocked and mortified. But he stopped it, never referred to it again and was as warmly supportive as ever to the woman working with him. He just kept his hands to himself thereafter.

Each of the individuals took a different course of action. What I found interesting was that none of them started with the obvious and simple course of action: indicating with quiet firmness that they didn't enjoy or find acceptable what was going on and wanted it stopped. The Jewish woman, for example, could have listened to the latest anti-Semitic joke and then spoken up: 'Let's move on to jokes about soccer players or another group,' she could have said. 'Because the Jewish stuff may seem very funny to you lot, but it isn't funny at the receiving end. Trust me.'

Nipping offensiveness in the bud is effective. Brooding about it, taking it personally, hoping someone will notice that you're taking it personally and amend their ways, is not. Make your point with humour, directness – and speedily move on to some other issue so you don't create a context where nobody knows what to do next. If the offensive behaviour was just the ill-judged action of a social dyslexic or a corporate culture needing a swift kick, those involved can change without getting defensive.

Telling your direct boss about it is another useful step. If, for example, your boss doesn't know that Harry from Accounts is known as Harry the Hand for good reason, then it's important he or she gets the information. If they don't tell Harry to keep his hands off female colleagues in the lift (which seems to be a recurring harassment zone), then they're complicit. Some organisations with a clearly articulated workplace policy have a nominated person to deal with this kind of issue. Go to them. But make sure you have your evidential ducks in a row.

It is very important for the harassed person or person who believes themselves to be harassed to keep a record of the individual incidents as they happen, ideally in diary format. Each individual incident can seem small in isolation but when occurring repeatedly can present an entirely different picture. It is the duty of the company to safeguard employees from acts of bullying or harassment and companies need to ensure that they have regular training of their employees to ensure buy-in to the company policies governing workplace behaviour.

It's worth stressing that bullying isn't once-off behaviour. If your boss loses it the day you fail to produce the response to a major request for tenders on time and bellows at you, it may be hurtful. It may be an affront to your dignity but it doesn't fit into a negative pattern. Regular humiliation does fit into a negative pattern. It can take the form of ridicule or belittling. It can also involve verbal abuse or use of obscene language. Unnecessarily commenting on the appearance of another person also counts. Bullying can occur in many guises, either in direct and obvious ways or in indirect and subtle forms. Bullying can also be a learned behaviour, particularly in a workplace where it is not detected and dealt with by the employer. A culture may exist within certain companies which lends itself to bullying being more easily tolerated or going unchecked.

Sexual harassment, on the other hand, is any form of unwanted verbal, non-verbal or physical conduct of a sexual nature. In contrast with bullying, one incident *can* amount to sexual harassment, which can take the form of rape jokes, of standing too close to a colleague, pursuing that colleague for a date or sex when the colleague has given no indication that they're interested in either, sticking up an offensive poster or circulating e-mails sharing details − fiction or fact − of that person's sexual performance or preference. It can be as simple − and offensive − as a whistle.

It' s not always necessary to make a formal or even an informal complaint if someone's behaviour is offensive to you. You may find it possible to start with quietly stating your case, without imputing vile intent to the offender. He or she may have no clue that you don't buy in to what's going on and that you find it personally offensive. Make sure when you try to put a stop to any behaviour you don't find acceptable that you do it on the way to something else.

Here's the wrong way to do it: 'I find those signs on the partitions personally offensive and would appreciate if they were taken down.'

Here's the right way to do it: 'I find those signs on the partitions personally offensive and I'm sure many of us do. If me and Robert were to take them down and replace them with these work-planners, it would prevent the double-booking that happened last week. While we're doing it, any chance someone'd get coffee for us all us?'

The second way moves people along. The first puts them in an awkward position. Salespeople call the second methodology 'sale by assumption'. Built into it is the assumption that every reasonable man and woman present wants the signs down, which takes those who really liked them off the hook. But it also gives people something to do, instead of leaving them in an embarrassing and threatening situation they will resent, with the possibility that, down the line, they will morph that resentment into dislike of the person who caused it. You.

Getting people to do the right thing is rarely achieved by condemning them for doing the wrong thing. Assume the best of your colleagues and they will usually live up to it.

But let's say this doesn't work or isn't appropriate, or the person making the complaint feels unable to tackle the situation in this direct and informal way. Many people who believe themselves to be victims of harassment and or bullying in the workplace feel unable to confront their situation in this manner. What then? It is your option to decide which procedure is most suitable for the situation in which you find yourself.

The Codes of Practice mentioned earlier respect and recognise the fact that a person should, as a general rule, make an attempt to address an issue of bullying or harassment as informally as possible by means of an agreed informal procedure. The objective of this approach is 'to resolve the difficulty with the minimum of conflict and stress for the individual concerned'.

If the informal procedure is not for you for whatever reason or if the problem persists, you should then make a formal complaint in writing to your supervisor or any member of management. A HR person is often designated to be the recipient of such written complaints and they will explain the procedures to you.

The important thing to remember, if you believe that you are being bullied or harassed, is that you have rights. You should seek help within your company. Like most things in life, it is up to you to start the ball rolling.

14

WHY WOMEN DON'T TRUST OTHER WOMEN

*All the women help the other, by speaking about it,
airing their pain and allowing others to air theirs and
spit out what they've suffered…*
Anonymous victim of multiple gang rapes in 1945 Berlin

If you're a reader of popular women's novels, you know the score. A woman who is beautiful, clever and sexy gets the man all her pals wanted and then her best friend sleeps with him or she gets breast cancer or her baby falls out of a tree. One way or the other, her husband can't stick her any more and leaves her. At the same time, her father gets Alzheimer's, her house burns down and her brother totals her sports car. At this point, all the women in her life she wasn't that pleasant to before her misfortunes start to arrive in battalions, rally around, bringing her scones, herbal teas, scented oils and sympathy. This brings her to her senses and she realises she should have been a better person and also that women are the best friends you could have. Bring up the violins, bring down the curtain and bring your hands together in a big round of applause for the theory that women all love and trust each other, under the skin.

They don't, of course. Not really. No beautiful young woman has failed to harbour the thought, looking at the attractive husband of a slightly older woman: 'I could take him.' No woman in the workplace has failed to consider the possibility that her boss got where she is by sleeping with someone important. No female hasn't complimented a friend on a new hairdo or weight lost and hated them for looking good. Every female lets on to be thrilled when a female friend is praised but even the warmest and most generous woman would prefer if the person being praised was a man.

Women are loyal to men, not to women. Men assume that it's a species-trait: women are just not as clubbable and decently laddish as men are. They'll tell you up straight:

> A fella can have a knock-down drag-out row with another fella and then go off for a pint with him. But a woman? Jasus, if a woman has a fight with another woman, particularly in the workplace, they start inviting everybody to join one of the two opposing camps, they get into conspiracies, they sulk for months, they inflate a bog-standard conflict of personality into something much more sinister. Women never just get over it. And that's because women basically don't like or trust each other.

Now, if women, in the past, had gone through a huge trauma that traumatised and scarred them, as a gender, right down to the present day, you could buy into that conceit. And in reality, women did, once, go through their own Holocaust. There's a case for suggesting that although history has largely forgotten it, a trace memory lingers in the gender ever since, skewing the relationship between one woman and another.

Women, in the early middle ages, were powerful. They created abbeys, some of which even had their own coinage. They were successful writers. They were herbalists and healers. They were powerful, influential and financially competent. One historian observed that 'the most remarkable aspect of this period was that men, for the most part, gracefully accepted women doing and women knowing'.

Then, everything changed.

Pope Innocent VIII was concerned about witchcraft. He appointed two men to root it out of Germany. These men, Heinrich Kramer and James Sprenger, wrote a book called *Malleus Maleficarum* (*The Hammer of Witches*) as an operating manual for witch-hunters. That was in 1486. The book made it clear why women – in the view of the two authors – were particularly likely to become witches.

'Three vices appear to have special dominion over wicked women, namely, infidelity, ambition and lust,' it said. 'Therefore they are more than others inclined toward witchcraft, who more than others are given to these vices.'

What became known as 'the witch craze' started small, in the fifteenth century. It started with the obvious candidates: deranged old women nobody liked and herbalists who, in addition to their knowledge of how to heal diseases and assist at childbirth, were suspected of creating concoctions to poison wells on the lands of people they didn't like. Irish dental surgeon, David Harris, says that the profile of the stereotypical witch we see at Hallowe'en displays is the sad end result of the loss of a woman's teeth:

> When a woman loses her teeth, her face falls in, her chin points upward and her nose, drawn by gravity, turns down towards her chin. That's because losing her teeth meant bone-loss as well – shrinkage of

the jaw bone. Until we had the capacity to do teeth implants, that was a reality faced by the majority of women – and it undoubtedly was a visual cue for the torture and execution of thousands of women in their middle years during the witch frenzy.

Once they had done away with the old women with their collapsed faces, the witch-finders moved on to younger women. The craze reached its height in the sixteenth century, and some historians believe it may have killed a million women. Which, given the much smaller population of Europe at the time, puts it right up there with the Holocaust in terms of destruction of the innocents in the most cruel way possible.

No woman was safe. A woman with the misfortune to have a birthmark, an unsightly mole or a deformity of any kind would find herself described as carrying the mark of the devil. A woman with exceptional beauty would be found guilty for another reason. The simplest of pleasures at the time – the company of a black pet cat – was enough to put some women into the ducking stool and on to the bonfires.

Very quickly, women worked out which were the best ways to avoid condemnation and execution. Keeping your mouth shut when your husband beat you or argued with you was one way. Being obedient, quiet and shy, so that nobody noticed you much, was another. Steering clear of female friendships was a third.

If a woman wanted to stay alive during the witch craze, the one thing she never showed was ambition or independence. As she watched women she knew to be the medical experts of her time scream through the flames as they died, she knew that to learn any of their expertise was dangerous. As she watched women condemned because they could tell stories or carve statues out of wood die in the same way, she knew that to be exceptionally talented or beautiful was dangerous. As male Europe, spurred on by Rome, annihilated the wise women of the time, it also turned the few survivors of torture into pariahs, wandering and begging. Rapes markedly increased, although rape trials decreased, as violent men figured out that if the woman they attacked took legal action against them, all they had to do was accuse her of witchcraft and they were home free. It was the only time in history, before or since, that the majority of the prisoners awaiting trial in jails all over Europe were women, not men.

The witch craze left many towns and villages without any women. It left whole swatches of Europe depopulated, when it came to one gender. Then it was quickly forgotten, except, bizarrely, in the happy-clappy yearly celebration of Hallowe'en, when children dress up as witches, wearing masks mimicking the fallen-in faces that caused thousands of wise, skilled women to be exterminated. It was forgotten for the obvious reasons that: a) most of the clever literate women were dead; and b) any who stayed alive were not going to endanger themselves by publishing the horror story of what had happened to their mothers, grandmothers, sisters and cousins.

But they would have passed on the lessons to their own daughters and their daughters would have learned from watching them. The lessons of the witch craze were that ambition and lust are OK in a man, but evil in a woman. That to be smart and to know healing secrets is OK in a man, but unacceptable in a woman. That to carry the signs of age is to become unacceptable, to become a lesser, even a disposable human being. That to fully trust another woman is dangerous, because even if she loves you, she'll tell lies about you under torture. She will deny those lies as soon as they stop burning her or breaking her back on the wheel or shoving her underwater in the medieval version of 'water-boarding' but you are safer not to trust her in the first place. A man may kill you. A woman may betray you to him...

The destruction of women throughout Europe (including Ireland) during the sixteenth century created a new culture of womanhood. Because survival required subservience, women learned to be subservient. They learned to be self-effacing, to express themselves through safe polite arts and crafts and to vent their discontents through enjoying bad health, whether that took the form of 'the vapours' in Victorian times, hysterical paralysis or addiction to the many versions of heroin and cocaine freely available to them in bottles described as 'female tonics'. They retreated into convents, where at least they could have careers, albeit at the cost of a sex life. And, generation after generation, they taught their daughters that marrying a good man, producing his children and maintaining a neat clean home was the priority.

Any time it looked as if they might break free of the deeply-embedded fear of being exceptional, ambitious or freely sexual, the Church herded them back into what it had decided was their proper place: in the home. Sometimes – as in Franco's Spain or Nazi Germany – the state got in on the act, defining the correct role for women as 'children, home and Church'.

When women told the truth about their lives, they suffered for it. One young journalist was in Berlin when it fell to the Red Army. This bright, travelled, independent and ambitious woman spent the last weeks before the German surrender in a bomb shelter. As soon as the guns went silent, the rapes started, as historian Anthony Beavor has recorded in his stunning book about the fall of Berlin. The young woman was repeatedly raped by Russian soldiers.

Starving, humiliated and desperately fearful of pregnancy or venereal disease or both, she kept herself sane by keeping a daily diary. (See 'The Ten Books you Need to Read', p. 204.) In an abandoned notebook she'd found in a derelict building, writing by candle-light with a pencil stub, she recorded the grim choices she made, based on intelligent analysis of what was happening to her. She could be raped by every passing Russian, or she could attach herself to an officer, knowing that serving as his concubine would provide protection against repeated alcohol-fuelled gang-rapes. That's what she did. Her Red Army lover used her, protected her, fed her – and moved on. She replaced him with another.

Her account of her life in the destroyed city was published in 1953. Anonymously. It was the story of women who survived starvation, disease, violent rape and slave labour. And it was condemned on all sides in her native land, which wanted to forget the horrors of the Third Reich as quickly as possible. Men didn't want to read about their women having been raped and about their failure to protect them. Women wanted to develop amnesia about a period they had suffered through – or, if they hadn't suffered through it, didn't want to know about it. The book disappeared and the author refused to consider reissuing it until after her death. We still don't know who she was, but we know that she represented a cohort of clever survivors; exceptional women whose practical approach to staying alive made pariahs of them.

Even in free America, in the sixties, when Women's Liberation started, the most savage attacks on the new generation of feminists were made by other women. Some of them were condemned for being ugly, some (like Gloria Steinem) were condemned for being too attractive. The real problem was that they were vocal, ambitious, uppity women who didn't know their place.

No wonder, despite the legislation that defines women as equal to men, that some women still feel the need to apologise for their ambition and still feel the pull of docile domesticity. And no wonder we trust each other much less willingly than men trust each other.

However, what every working woman needs to know is that women are not inherently treacherous or underhand. In bad times, they can be your best supporter.

What we need to learn – still – is the capacity to give generous support to the exceptions among us. The ones who are uppity, argumentative, ambitious and lustful.

Who don't know their place. And never will.

15

Women and Money:
Shopping, Saving and Pensions

*I love clothes. I can't control myself. I have a huge
fetish for shoes and clothes and make-up. I'm the kind
of person who doesn't like to wear things over and over
again.*

Hilary Duff

If you can't imagine getting through a week without a shopping
expedition, get yourself a job as a personal shopper. Because if
you want to become a serious player, whether in managing your
own company or getting to the top in the organisation in which
you work, it's what you do at work that should define you, not
the kick you get out of stretching your credit card to the limit
and leaving the shopping centre with six big square bags filled
with shoes, bags and other paraphernalia.

If shopping is the new religion, as a working woman you
need to be an atheist. Go shopping for clothes twice a year at
most, with a budget you won't exceed. Buy what you need, not
what you want. Make sure it's coordinated. And then quit.

When you meet friends, don't meet them in shopping malls
or in a situation where comparison of purchases made is the

order of the day. Get over the shopping urge. It costs time and money and concentration and it never satisfies. The purchase that was going to make you feel good forever makes you feel good for a day and a half, and then the credit card charge comes in and you feel miserable.

Many executive women get sent by their company on time management courses where they learn the obvious (for example, that the urgent tends to take the place of the important) and which change their lives not one bit. One of the reasons is that those courses rarely address the time *surrounding* the time spent at work. But it's the management of this time that distinguishes successful working women from the ones who are always tired, always behind their schedule, always slightly scatty.

Shopping for clothes only twice a year is one step. Grocery shopping once a month is another. Vast quantities of constantly-required items can be – indeed, should be – bulk-purchased. Bottles or cans of drinks, cans of soup, pasta and rice, partly-baked breads, jars of jam, bars of soap, bottles of shampoo, shaving foam, dishwasher and washing-machine detergent can be stockpiled. The more you reduce the number of times you visit Tesco or Superquinn, the more you reduce the temptation to buy calorific rubbish you know you really don't need or want.

Fill your freezer, not with what you like, but with what your family actually eats. If you cook, cook twice as much as is going to be eaten and freeze the other half with a label on it carrying instructions on how to defrost and cook. If this latter seems a bit excessive, here's an example of what happened one of my colleagues. She left a Tupperware container filled with delicious casserole in the fridge with a note on it instructing her husband, very simply, 'Heat the oven to 200 and cook.' He did. They were picking stalactites of melted Tupperware off the bars of the oven shelves for weeks.

Involve other people in the remainder of the shopping. Men are good at shopping, particularly if you give them a list. So the items you need purchased fresh during the week can be picked up at Centra or Supervalu, where you don't have to pay parking fees for every hour spent in the store. Or shop on the Internet and make sure someone is at home when the van arrives to deliver it.

Plan ahead. Each year has particular periods when the demands on the household budget radically increase. Pre-Christmas is such a period, as are the stretches before an overseas holiday, the time before Easter and coming up to a wedding.

The financial impact of some of those exigencies tends to be under-estimated. Ruhama, the group of religious who offer services to sex workers in our cities, say that one of the times of the year which sees an increase of women going onto the streets is the spring. It happens because mothers can see no other way to pay for the Holy Communion outfits to make their daughters look like miniature brides.

For the working woman, the money and time spent on shopping should be a manageable issue, not a series of Toblerone peaks and troughs creating anxieties that seep into the working day.

Young working women don't want to know about two aspects of money. They don't want to know about saving and they don't want to think about pensions. It's a little bit like wills. Any solicitor will tell you that people who have a strong view on what they want to happen to their home and other property after they snuff it, nevertheless don't get around to dealing with the matter of making a will because of an atavistic fear that making a will might in some way cause them to die sooner.

In the same way, young people get the shudders when the very word 'pension' is mentioned. It comes with 'toupee' and 'false teeth' in the list of possibilities implicit in getting older that they simply do not wish to consider for a moment.

Let's start with saving. Many working women end up setting money aside each month in a negative way: to pay off a car loan. So what's the problem about doing it positively? Having a good credit rating is a great force for stress-reduction. Having a secret stash of money to serve as the deposit on a house, for example, means you are much more likely to get a mortgage, and – even more important – that when you get it, it doesn't cripple you for the following years.

Pensions are an even more important issue. This book is not the place to outline the different models of pension. Your company may make full provision or may have a model that requires supplementation by you.

The reality is that putting money into a pension is quite simply the most tax-effective way of using the cash you get each month. You may not, in your early twenties, actually believe you will reach sixty or sixty-five or whatever age will coincide with your retirement, any more than, viscerally, you believe you will die. But you will reach that age and you will feel the two ends of a fool if you were hoping the senior citizen pension would allow you to maintain the standard of living you currently enjoy.

'I'd be spending much less, at that point,' I hear you say. 'The house would be paid off and I wouldn't be travelling as much.'

Says who? Travel has become more rather than less of an option for older people. If you hit sixty and find yourself in the whole of your health, who says you will suddenly be content with a boring, stay-at-home life that costs little to sustain? The chances are that you will want to do all the fun things you postponed during your active working life. That requires money. More money than €12,000 a year – and that's the current level of the state pension,.

The earlier you start funding a pension, the less painful it is. Commit to a small amount every month, leave it alone no matter how tight your finances and you will, decade by decade, build up a worthwhile pension fund. Go to the web site of the Pensions Board if you want to know more.

If you have a friend who's good with figures and finances (an accountant or tax expert, or even better, an actuary) ask their advice. Not just about how you should approach your pension, but about who should handle it for you. The women I talked to who were happiest with their pension arrangements had people they trusted on the task. The women who were unhappiest had people they thought they could trust on the task, only to find out that their level of trust did not turn out to be justified, or – in the case of one working woman – that the person she thought had been handling her account had in fact retired:

> I entrusted my pension fund to a partner in one of the big financial services firms. He worked out a series of investments for different sections of the money, I was happy and I left it with him. Every now and then I'd get reports but I wouldn't pay that much attention to them, because I trusted him and felt, as a result, that I didn't need to personally parse every incoming report.

Then came the global sub-prime lending disaster and economic turndown. She was even busier than normal because of having to sustain her mid-sized company against dropping international market share and a rake of other complications, so didn't give her pension much thought. Then a friend who had dealt with the same man telephoned her to ask if she'd talked with him recently.

'No. Why?'

'He's dealing with your pension, right?'

'Right. Why?'

'Because I've just found out my pension is in rag order and when I called them to talk to him, I also found out he had retired. I ate the face off them for not telling me, and they simply said they provided a seamless service and partner X was now in charge of my account.'

When the second woman called the partnership, she found her own pension fund's value had also dropped. Severely. When she evinced rage at this, they pointed out that they sent out bulletins at regular intervals. She believed they were taking care of her money and should have contacted her – in person, on the phone or at a meeting – the moment it started to lose value. They believed she should have read the routine material they sent her. Both women moved their funds and hired somebody they could trust to stay actively managing their money, instead of the prestigious company that had, in their view, stood idly by while large amounts of the monies which they had been planning to provide them with a decent income in their old age went down the tubes.

The lesson is to understand fully what you expect and what professionals normally deliver. If you want a heads-up in the event of changes in the market that might affect your funds, make sure to build that into your agreement with them. If you're happy to get printed quarterly reports, the standard operational approach will work for you.

Make sure your financial adviser knows the totality of your situation. One company I was advising discovered, too late, the concept of 'Key Man Insurance,' although in their case, it should have been 'Key Woman Insurance'. They found this out when their MD developed brittle diabetes that took almost a year to stabilise. During that year, the company was in chaos. Although a replacement was found, the MD was also the founder of the company, which presented enormous problems and cost money because so much of the company's memory was stored in her brain cells. Key Man Insurance would have greatly helped them.

Similarly, a tax advisor who knows which perks – like the company paying for your bus pass – don't attract Benefit in Kind tax and which perks – like the company paying for a free parking space for you – do attract BIK can be very helpful when it comes to ensuring you avoid unnecessary tax. And no, I am not suggesting cheating the tax woman (the top bod in the Revenue Commissioners, I'm glad to tell you, is a woman.)

Avoiding tax is legal. It's when you *evade* tax you go to jail.

16

Families, Aged Parents and Other Distractions

Happy families are all alike; every unhappy family is unhappy in its own way.

Leo Tolstoy, *Anna Karenina*

Families have always found reasons to prove wrong the warm cuddly feelings emanating from the phrase 'family life'. From the very beginning. Think of Cain and Abel. One of them killed the other because the other got a better response from God to a present he gave him.

Families fight over money, inheritance, one another's behaviours, perceived insults, lack of appreciation by one member of the children of another member, disapproval of the chosen mate of one sibling by another sibling, one being favoured over another by a parent or parents – you name it, families fight about it. Not only do they fight about it, they stop speaking to each other for months or years or a whole lifetime.

That's been complicated in recent years by relationship breakdown and second relationships. Grandparents have taken their own children to court in order to get visiting rights to the grandkids. Even if it doesn't go that far, when a relationship breaks down, family members try to intervene, sometimes with lethal consequences.

'I just thought I should talk sense to my brother about his ridiculous affair,' one woman says. 'He hasn't spoken to me since and won't let me talk to my godson.'

What's interesting about this fairly typical example is that the man probably doesn't think about his sister at all, whereas no day passes without his sister grieving about the fact that she isn't in contact with that side of her family. Women always hope to find a way to repair a family rift. Men seem to manage to get on with their lives without giving it much attention, whereas women spend time examining their feelings, the rights and wrongs of the situation and the guilt or blame accruing.

Families are like what Churchill said about democracy. They're a seriously flawed way to manage human relations, but nobody's come up with anything better, thus far.

One of the realities facing many working women is that, having postponed having their children until their thirties, when they hit their late forties, they find themselves coping simultaneously with the trauma of adolescent offspring and parents in their seventies or older, who may be suffering from Alzheimer's.

The statistics indicate that most people who reach their seventies will live happy, healthy, independent lives for a decade or more thereafter. The statistics also indicate that adolescents, in the main, become human beings a decade later. But when you're the working woman caught between the worst possibilities, the statistics of the general situation are no consolation.

The best advice I ever got about adolescent offspring I quoted in an earlier book, *The Best Advice I Ever Got*. It's worth repeating, here. Máire Geoghegan-Quinn, then a government minister, now attached to the EU in Luxembourg, told me that when your son (or daughter) is fifteen or sixteen, someone takes them away from your house and sticks a horrible lookalike in their place. This lookalike (depending on how lucky or unlucky you are) is surly, won't get out of bed, drinks, smokes, takes drugs and has sex with inappropriate people in inappropriate places, doesn't come home at night, won't study, won't keep themselves clean, won't help around the house, throws parties whenever you're not there and thinks their parents, particularly their mother, are the most boring, tedious uncool humans ever born, requiring sullen rudeness at all times.

MGQ said the good side of this general picture is that, when the kid hits nineteen or twenty, they take back the godawful substitute and return your own kid. Believe it. It usually happens. Anyway, you have no choice. Short of chaining your daughter to the wall and putting an electronic ankle-bracelet on her to track her every move, you can't prevent a sixteen or seventeen-year old from making the mistakes they ache to make, commit the sins you know you committed yourself at the same age, and reap the dire consequences. That the dire consequences will affect you and the rest of the family is a grim side issue. That's life.

Not only will the law not permit you to chain your daughter to the wall, it won't do anything about your son's various nasty behaviours. Nor can you, especially if you're reasonably short and your son is a fit, well-built six footer.

The fascinating fact which emerged in talking with working women who are successful in career terms is that something stops them applying to their families the skills and instincts which bring them workplace achievement. Women who are clinically-focused on the bottom line, who make ruthless unsentimental decisions about the deployment of staff and who take no shit from superiors, colleagues or clients become conflicted, guilt-ridden, emotional and incapable when it comes to coping with the problems families pose to the middle-aged.

The problem is that in human relations, no guarantees apply, no matrices matter, no review systems are apposite. In many situations, there's no 'right' answer, only an 80 per cent right answer.

Women get eaten alive by a sense of duty and responsibility to their parents – and rightly so, in one sense. These are the people who – if you had a close family – stood by you when your marriage broke up or you had a miscarriage or failed to get the promotion on which you had set your heart. They minded your children and gave you chunks of freedom and relaxation. They were always looking out for you. How could you, now, do that awful thing: put them in a home?

Some women put extensions on their home, bring their aged parents into the extra space and hire people to help. One company, called Home Instead (www.homeinstead.ie), specialises in providing the graduated support needed to help older people live at home or with their children as independently as possible for as long as possible. Their services start with the simple and occasional, working up to much more regular and comprehensive responses.

The thing to do, of course, is to research all the options along with your parents long before the exigency arises. None of the women I talked to had done this. Some because they hadn't thought of it. Some because they knew their parents would regard it in much the same way as people see making a will: a harbinger of disaster, dissolution and death. Some don't do it because their parents are strong, healthy and ultra-independent until the day Dad has a major stroke, quickly followed by Ma breaking her hip, creating total chaos.

'I spent a year rushing from one hospital to another,' one woman told me. 'My father couldn't talk and couldn't understand why my mother wasn't with him. My mother was so determined to be with him, she kept fighting with the hospital staff and putting her recovery back.'

Their daughter found herself in a morass of competing miseries. In each of the hospitals, she found herself beset by social workers, who wanted her parents to move to step-down facilities. Separate step-down facilities. Her immediate family began to resent how much she was absent and how hassled she was when she was present. Her two brothers, one in England, managed to visit about one tenth as often as she did, yet were welcomed by her parents with much more enthusiasm than she was. They also gave her a lot of free advice as to what she should do but took no direct part in finding a solution themselves, restricting themselves to whingeing about the choices she was about to make and wondering aloud if it wouldn't be better if their parents went to live with her.

She made the decisions and lived with the sense of failure and with the thwarted desire to kill her two brothers and her eldest daughter, who demonstrated a level of self-involvement during that period which astonished her mother. It didn't help that the girl's father took the daughter's side on every occasion, making her mother feel betrayed and isolated. All the while, she was running a large organisation that was going through a major transition phase. Looking back on it now she says:

> I would honestly say the only thing I did right, throughout the entire process, was not to move house. A house we'd always wanted came on the market at

the time, we went to look at it, were enthusiastic about it, and then I – unilaterally, I have to say – just did a 'Whoa'. Meaning that moving house is an incredibly stressful task, even if you've nothing else going on. I remember reading somewhere that it's one of the stressors that added to others, can increase your chance of an early death. I wasn't really afraid of dying but I knew I just couldn't cope with one more hassle. Because I've always been the coper in the family. I delegate at work, not at home. So I've become the one to be relied on in the family, which – trust me – is not where you want to be at fifty-six when everything starts to collapse on top of you. Everybody's so used to you getting the act together that they just expect you to get on with it, no matter what other shit you have to deal with at the same time.

Some women who have come through this particularly difficult phase in a working woman's life tend to offer spectacularly unhelpful advice, like: 'Pick a great partner twenty years earlier.' Others suggest rigid segmentation of time. One said:

I realised I had to ring-fence the time I spent dealing with my mother, the nursing home, her visits to hospital, selling the family house and coping with overseas siblings. Otherwise it was going to overflow into every hour of every day. Give an example. My mother has since died, and I have yet to go through her old papers, photographs and diaries, because I made the decision that they wouldn't go away and had no immediate relevance to what I was doing.

> In retrospect, I realise I'd have been emotionally
> upset by what I found, so I gained two ways by
> postponement.

Making decisions and deciding to live with them, putting
guilt and second-guessing to one side, is another good practice.
As is indicating to other relatives that they have a choice: they
can take over the task or belt up about how you manage it.

One woman who had experienced a cluster of these
simultaneous mid-life crises got up in the middle of the night
because she was sleepless. Sitting at the kitchen table clutching
a mug of herbal tea, she began to cry, all by herself. 'D'you know
when crying isn't for show, but it's still noisy and abject? It just
took me over. I put my head down on my arms and cried and
cried.'

When a hand began to stroke her shoulder, she was too
exhausted to leap in surprise. After a few minutes, she sniffled
and dried her eyes and sat up, to find that the back-stroker was
her teenage son, on his way back – way too late – from a date.

> Normally, I'd've eaten the face off him and he'd have
> been horrible back to me, but this time I just told
> him all the complications and he listened quietly and
> gave me the best advice anybody could have. It was
> a turning point for the two of us. He didn't convert
> to perfection but he did do quiet helpful things. The
> things it suited him to do, not the things I might have
> wanted him to do. But helpful anyway. And I suppose
> I realised that I was missing out on a resource. I was
> always giving him advice. It never struck me that,
> coming from a position of pig-ignorance, he might

be able to look at the problem with more objectivity than I could.

As with all the speed-bumps in a working woman's life, the same principles apply:

- Don't talk/think about your feelings. Just address the data and decisions.
- Don't waste time on anger or guilt. They're counter-productive.
- Don't abandon your fitness regimen.
- Don't abandon your life and your friends.
- When your adolescents are driving you crazy, resign from motherhood and become their aunt instead. Mothers are interventive, needy, ever-present, hypercritical and controlling. Aunts are easy-going and don't pay that much attention but notice achievements and foster potential.
- Keep it simple. Better to lose a little money than a chunk of your precious life.

Oh, and one other thing. Look forward to your own later years and plan for the worst, not the best. Grim and pessimistic? Not at all. Airbags go into cars to plan for the worst. That doesn't prevent most of us buying gorgeous cars and having a lot of fun driving them.

You can have more fun driving the later years of your working life if you've put in the airbags to take care of negative eventualities.

One final thought.

On the really bad nights, when you awake lie in bed, resentful of the sounds of your partner's contented sleep, fearful of the concatenation of factors coming together to remove your money, sanity, promotion, looks, diet and health, visualise the lot of them going on to a bonfire and you setting fire to them.

And then whisper a little promise to yourself.

'Tomorrow will be better…'

17

YOU'RE NEVER TOO OLD…

The tragedy of old age is not that one is old, but that one is young.

Oscar Wilde

It's more than a lack of respect: older people in Ireland are as despised as any racial minority

Every year, some plank rings to tell me that a newspaper (usually the *Sunday Independent*) has me listed in their birthdays-of-the-week box. Exposing my precise age to the public. Down to the very day. As a result, I can't let on to be younger than I am.

Marlene Deitrich used to pull the wrinkles out of her face by hauling all loose skin to the back of her head and sticking a hat-pin through it. Clap a beret on the top of it and that was ten years lopped off, no problem. But there's not much point in hat-pinning ten years off if anybody who reads the paper can find out how old you really are.

On the good side, though, I do have a job. For as long as I'm competent and eager to work. With as many career options as anybody could want. Unlike the increasing number of executives, male and female, in their forties and fifties who turn up at my company every week, desperately seeking ways around the active ageism within their organisations that is crippling their careers.

Long before Ryanair fell foul of the Equality Agency for coming out and saying, in print recruitment ads, that they were looking for 'young, vibrant' employees, I had witnessed enough real-life case studies to be clear that Ireland is the most unashamedly ageist country in Europe, if not the world.

In the private sector, women come for consultation because they're coming under benign pressure to take early retirement. Benign as in: 'Take the good package or be sidelined into Long-Term Strategic Planning where you can retain a desk and title, plus have the fun of producing documents nobody will ever read.'

In the public sector, they go hopelessly forward for promotion interviews, murmuring resignedly about having gone as far as they're going to get in the civil service, because 'the emphasis these days is on getting younger women'. The resignation is the worst aspect of it. It's as though they have bought into the prejudice: 'Well, nobody wants an old bag of forty-five, do they? You know how it is.'

Feeding into that grim resignation is the experience of hundreds of women who never get responses to CVs which demonstrably meet the specs of the job advertised, and some of whom later find a younger, less qualified person being appointed.

Even when called to interview, highly competent women find themselves anxiously trying to prove energy and intellectual flexibility to interviewers who clearly assume that both diminish after forty.

In the more clued-in, cautious companies, no offensive questions are asked. In the more up-front operations, ageism is recklessly apparent in questions which effectively ask the applicant to prove herself innocent of the failings of older people.

And you know what? The owners of the prejudices are comfortably certain that their prejudices are fact.

Just as, thirty years ago, their predecessors were sure a woman couldn't captain a big passenger jet (you'd be taking your life in your hands, she'd be so hysterical coming up to her period) or read the news on TV (nobody'd hear what she was saying, they'd be fancying her so much).

They miss the point about equality in recruitment. It's competence you should be looking for, at any age. Not age.

But then, expecting the age-chauvinists to be any different, when they're surrounded on all sides by rampant reinforcement, is unrealistic.

For years, they've been listening to politicians of all hue, prating on about X per cent of our population being under twenty-five, as if that meant we were blessed, compared to countries weighed down with old farts in their late thirties and early forties.

For years, they've been listening to propaganda linking achievement, education, drive and energy exclusively to young people.

Pushed, they may acknowledge that there *are* energetic task-oriented achievers in their sixties, and that some executives are burned-out bores at thirties. But those are the exceptions, they state, basing their belief that older people are all 'inflexible tedious control freaks who can't use computers' on their least-liked parent or most-hated teacher.

To be over forty, in Ireland, right now, is to spend every day walking into overt, repeated, crudely expressed, infinitely wounding prejudices. Not only is there nothing positive in the way mass media tackle ageing; there's nothing even neutral in the way mass media observes the outward and visible signs.

The deadly verdict is often delivered in captions under pictures in newspapers and magazines, its negativity obvious and presumably editorially approved. 'The ageing Brigitte Bardot,' the caption will run, delivering a sweeping backhand smack.

Of course, I hear you say, that reflects the prejudices out there in the market place. Too right. You could listen out forever in the hope of comments like: 'See the wisdom in that woman's face. Look at the lovely wrinkles, isn't she much more beautiful at sixty than she was at thirty?'

You sometimes hear that kind of comment about men. Never about women. Not by the wildest stretch of imagination could 'ageing' be considered a positive description. In some other century maybe, but at a time when sexiness is everything, 'ageing' means the opposite, carrying connotations of a flaccid decay and pallid sagginess.

Not so long ago, I overheard a banter session led by men but not excluding women. The subject? Whether a woman's face ages as fast or faster than her cleavage. The men present gave millimetre-precise distinctions between the young cleavage and the old.

How unacceptable the old cleavage might be was a given, rather than a topic for debate. It was the age giveaway. No matter how a woman acts or exercises or dresses, once you saw the cleavage you could tell her age, practically to the year. Like rings in a tree trunk.

The implication was: either you get your old bits fixed or you conceal them. Older women, ran the sub-text, should know their place and their place is to be invisible.

Marilyn Monroe said that once you were famous, people

assumed you stopped having feelings. The same judgement is made when you start to age. With an added refinement: not only are you assumed to have no feelings – it's assumed you have no right to have feelings. Bad enough to be a wrinklie, but a wrinklie without a sense of humour about being mentioned in print as a market segment nobody'd be caught dead with?

For the first time in history, Ireland is going to join the US, Japan and other countries in containing a mass population of long-lived elderly men and women at a time when every day, in thousands of ways, again and again, we are being influenced to like what's young and dislike what's old.

Never mind political correctness: we're up to our armpits in gerontophobia – the fear/hatred of old people.

It will be a long time before we see, in Ireland, a sign like the one carried on a medical supplies company in Massachusetts: 'Help wanted. Light machine operators. Part-time. Employees set own hours/days. Predominantly senior citizens. *No* retirement age.'

The company owning the sign at first employed older people with reluctance tempered by the knowledge that they were likely to be, at least, reliable and inexpensive. In time, their figures revealed that choosing to employ workers in their sixties was more cost-effective: they were more careful and tended to have only half as many work-related accidents as younger workers.

'Management also came to regard them as harder-working, more loyal, and less prone to personal problems than many younger workers,' one business commentator noted. 'The company's annual sales have grown by 20 per cent every year for the past five years. Average age of their employees: seventy-three.'

In the US, Travellers Insurance has been saved $1.5m a year

by the higher productivity of retired workers, hired back on a part-time basis. General Electric found it more economical to retrain veteran engineers in emerging technologies than to hire new ones. The Americans talk about a trend towards rehirement, rather than retirement.

Writing a novel a few years back, I ran into a problem. I wanted one of my characters to become a fire-fighter. As in a real, live, fire-brigade fire-fighter in America. Except the woman was hitting forty. I talked to the fire department. No problem, they said. Doesn't matter what age she is, as long as she can get through the physical tests. We don't discriminate against older people or smaller people. Legally, we're not allowed to. But it isn't a problem: if the individual is fit enough for the task, they're fit enough for the task. End of story.

Remember the days when young people emigrated in hordes to get US jobs?

Don't look now, but we're heading fast towards a day when older people head to the US in search of something that is even more essential. Equality. And tolerance.

18

The Ten Books You Need to Read
and Why You Need to Read Them

1. Michael Gaffney and Colin O'Brien. *That'll Never Work: Success Stories from Private Irish Business*. KPMG/Mercier, 2008.

The two KPMG partners who edited this book cleverly got out of the way of the entrepreneurs they selected to interview. So you get the story – of Celtic Bookmakers or Carton Chickens or the GreenCone – straight from the mouth and mind of the man or woman driving the business. The fact that women are in a minority is irrelevant: just dip into it to learn how super-successful people cope with triumph and disaster. And if you need a laugh, read Ivan Yates's account of how he got out of politics and into business along with his wife, Deirdre.

2. Judith Rich Harris. *The Nurture Assumption*. Free Press, 1999.

Anyone who feels overwhelmed by parenthood should read this book, because it will change the way you see parenting. Plus the writer is argumentative and entrepreneurial, coming from nowhere to challenge establishment thinking.

3. Deirdre Purcell. *Diamonds and Holes in My Shoes*. Hodder
    Headline Ireland, 2006.

Deirdre Purcell is a long-running success story. She started
acting with the Abbey, then acted in the US, then became a TV
newsreader, then a profile-writer for a Sunday newspaper and
finally a best-selling novelist. Easy peasy. Read this autobiography
to find out just how easy it wasn't. Deirdre is one of those people
who I suspect can't sleep at night if she hasn't done at least five
major good turns for other people during the day – I've been at
the receiving end. A dip into her life is instructive.

4. Terry Prone. *Talk the Talk*. Currach Press, 2007.
    Well, I would, wouldn't I?

5. Joan Didion. *The Year of Magical Thinking*. Knopf, 2005.

Joan Didion's writer husband died suddenly, severing a partnership going back to their youth and setting Didion adrift in grief,
numbed with shock. This is her lyrical account of the first year
of her bereavement.

6. Ori Brafman and Rom Brafman. *Sway: The Irresistible Pull
    of Irrational Behavior*. Doubleday NY, 2008.

Funny, interesting and useful background for any businesswoman.

7. Anonymous. *A Woman in Berlin* (Introduction by Anthony
    Beavor). Virago Press, 2005.

I mentioned this book already on pages 174 and 179-80. It's
about anti-heroism and how it kept one woman afloat in the
horrors of Berlin at the end of the Second World War.

8.   Gillian Gill. *Nightingales*. Random House, 2004.
A biography of Florence Nightingale and her less famous sister, this marvellous book knocks over the old reverential notion of Flo as 'The Lady with the Lamp,' moving quietly at night through the wards of the wounded in military hospitals during the Boer war. Instead the reader comes away with a picture of a tough, ambitious, powerful and merciless operator.

9.   Gavin de Becker. *Fear Less*. Little, Brown 2002.
A book about self-protection, safety and not denying the value of your own intuitive fears.

10.   John G. Murphy and Jason Dunne. *Inheritance and Succession: The Complete Irish Guide*. Liberties Press, 2008.
A sensible, understandable handbook by legal experts Murphy and Dunne about how to approach making a will.